麦格希 中英双语阅读文库

神话故事与传说

【美】史蒂芬·科斯格罗夫 (Stephen Cosgrove) ●主编

于俊男 苗迎雪 刘慧●译

麦格希中英双语阅读文库编委会●编

全国百佳图书出版单位
吉林出版集团股份有限公司

图书在版编目（CIP）数据

神话故事与传说 / (美) 史蒂芬·科斯格罗夫
(Stephen Cosgrove) 主编；于俊男，苗迎雪，刘慧译；麦格
希中英双语阅读文库编委会编. -- 2版. -- 长春：吉林
出版集团股份有限公司, 2018.3（2022.1重印）
（麦格希中英双语阅读文库）
ISBN 978-7-5581-4768-5

Ⅰ.①神… Ⅱ.①史… ②于… ③苗… ④刘… ⑤麦
… Ⅲ.①英语—汉语—对照读物②民间故事—作品集—世
界 Ⅳ.①H319.4：I

中国版本图书馆CIP数据核字(2018)第046437号

神话故事与传说

编：麦格希中英双语阅读文库编委会
插　画：齐　航　李延霞
责任编辑：王芳芳
封面设计：冯冯翼
开　本：660mm × 960mm　1/16
字　数：214千字
印　张：9.5
版　次：2018年3月第2版
印　次：2022年1月第2次印刷

出　版：吉林出版集团股份有限公司
发　行：吉林出版集团外语教育有限公司
地　址：长春市福祉大路5788号龙腾国际大厦B座7层
　　　　邮编：130011
电　话：总编办：0431-81629929
　　　　发行部：0431-81629927　0431-81629921(Fax)
印　刷：北京一鑫印务有限责任公司

ISBN 978-7-5581-4768-5　　定价：35.00元
版权所有　　侵权必究　　举报电话：0431-81629929

前 言 *PREFACE*

英国思想家培根说过：阅读使人深刻。阅读的真正目的是获取信息，开拓视野和陶冶情操。从语言学习的角度来说，学习语言若没有大量阅读就如隔靴搔痒，因为阅读中的语言是最丰富、最灵活、最具表现力、最符合生活情景的，同时读物中的情节、故事引人入胜，进而能充分调动读者的阅读兴趣，培养读者的文学修养，至此，语言的学习水到渠成。

"麦格希中英双语阅读文库"在世界范围内选材，涉及科普、社会文化、文学名著、传奇故事、成长励志等多个系列，充分满足英语学习者课外阅读之所需，在阅读中学习英语、提高能力。

◎难度适中

本套图书充分照顾读者的英语学习阶段和水平，从读者的阅读兴趣出发，以难易适中的英语语言为立足点，选材精心、编排合理。

◎精品荟萃

本套图书注重经典阅读与实用阅读并举。既包含国内外脍炙人口、耳熟能详的美文，又包含科普、人文、故事、励志类等多学科的精彩文章。

◎功能实用

本套图书充分体现了双语阅读的功能和优势，充分考虑到读者课外阅读的方便，超出核心词表的词汇均出现在使其意义明显的语境之中，并标注释义。

鉴于编者水平有限，凡不周之处，谬误之处，皆欢迎批评教正。

我们真心地希望本套图书承载的文化知识和英语阅读的策略对提高读者的英语著作欣赏水平和英语运用能力有所裨益。

丛书编委会

Contents

1

Story of the Sun

Long ago, a *curious* young boy lived in a far-off land.

To the east there were mountains.

To the west there was a large sea.

As each day began, the curious young boy sat and looked to the east. He watched the sun rise over the mountains.

As each day ended, he looked west.

He watched the sun *sink* into the sea.

The curious boy's name was Ichiro.

太阳的故事

很久以前，有个好奇心很强男孩住在遥远的岛上。

岛的东边是大山。

岛的西边是大海。

每天清晨男孩坐下来望着东方，看着太阳从山上升起。

每天晚上他望着西方，看着夕阳沉入大海。

男孩的名字叫铃木一郎。

---

curious *adj.* 好奇的；求知欲强的   sink *v.* 下沉

Ichiro wondered where the sun came from.

And he *wondered* where it went each night.

The harder Ichiro thought, the more *confused* he became.

He wondered how many suns there really are.

Would there ever be a time when a new sun would not rise from the east?

Ichiro was smart. He knew that the sun brought light.

He knew that without the sun, everything would be dark.

He also knew that the sun brought warmth.

He loved to feel the warm sun on his brown skin.

Ichiro worried about a day when a new sun might not rise.

铃木一郎想知道太阳每天早上从哪里来，晚上到哪去。

男孩越想越糊涂。

他想知道到底有多少个太阳。

会不会有一天太阳不从东方升起。

铃木一郎很聪明，他知道是太阳带来了光明。

他知道如果没有太阳，只能是漆黑一片。

他还知道是太阳带来了温暖。

他喜欢阳光晒在他棕色皮肤上温暖的感觉。

铃木一郎担心有一天太阳不会再升起。

---

wonder *v.* 想知道；想弄明白   confused *adj.* 糊涂的；迷惑的

He worried about living in a land of darkness.

He worried about being cold.

Ichiro learned about a wise old woman.

He was told she knew the answers to everything.

So he decided to visit her.

The wise woman lived in a village. The village was near the mountains. It was near where the sun rose each morning.

One morning Ichiro awoke early.

He climbed on his giant pet *emu* and rode *swiftly* to the east. In a few hours, he entered the village.

他担心住在漆黑的岛上。

他担心寒冷。

铃木一郎知道有一位聪明的老奶奶。

他听说老奶奶知道一切答案。

所以决定去拜访她。

聪明的老奶奶住在一个村庄里。村庄靠近大山，就是每天早上太阳升起的地方。

有一天，铃木一郎早上起得很早。

他骑上他的宠物———一只大鸸鹋，向东方飞奔而去。过了几个小时，

---

emu *n.* 鸸鹋   swiftly *adv.* 迅速地；敏捷地

3

The wise woman greeted Ichiro warmly.

She took him into her *hut*.

And she began to answer his questions about the sun.

First she explained where the sun came from.

"Do you see that large mountain? The one that is towering above all other mountains?" she asked, pointing east.

Ichiro replied, "Yes, I do. In fact I see the sun rise over that mountain each morning."

他来到了村庄。

老奶奶热情地迎接了铃木一郎。

带他走进自己的小屋。

然后开始回答他关于太阳的问题。

首先她解释了太阳来自哪里。

她指着东方，问道："你看见那座大山了吗？就是远远高于其他山的那座。"

铃木一郎回答说："看到了。其实每天早上我都看见太阳从那座山上升起。"

---

hut *n.* 简陋的小房子

"Well," said the wise woman, "that is where new suns come from. Each night after the sun sinks into the sea, people from the village go to the mountaintop. They carry large pieces of wood and *coal* with them."

"They drop the wood and coal into a large opening at the top of the mountain," she said.

"The mountain begins to *rumble*. It roars and smokes."

The wise old woman kept telling her story.

"By morning, the rumbling is very loud.

Then suddenly the mountain spits out a giant ball of fire.

The ball is spit out with great *force*.

聪明的老奶奶说："哦，那里就是新的太阳产生的地方。每天晚上太阳沉入大海以后，村庄里的人都去山顶。他们扛去很多大木头和煤炭。"

她说："他们把木头和煤炭运到山顶的一片大开阔地。"

"于是山开始隆隆作响和冒烟。"

聪明的老奶奶继续说道：

"到了早上，隆隆声变得很大。

突然间，大山喷出一个巨大的火球。

火球喷出时带有巨大的力量，被喷射到高高的天空中。跃上天空的火

---

coal *n.* 煤炭   rumble *v.* 发出隆隆声
force *n.* 力；力量

It shoots up high into the sky. The fireball lights the land below as it travels across the sky. It also heats the land."

"When the ball of fire reaches its highest point, it begins to drop," she continued. In a few hours it *crashes* into the sea. The cool waters of the sea put out the ball of fire."

"It is very important that the villagers go to the mountain each night. They must *feed* it wood and coal," she said.

"As long as we feed the mountain, it will make a new sun each morning. But if ever we fail to do so, there will be no new sun. Then the land will become dark and cold."

From that day on, Ichiro worried no more.

球照亮了下面的大地，给大地带来热量。"

她接着说道："当火球到达最高处以后，就开始下落了。几个小时后，火球沉入海里。冰凉的海水熄灭了火球。"

她说："人们每天晚上去山上是非常重要的，他们必须为大山提供木头和煤炭。"

"只要我们供养大山，每天早晨就会有新的太阳。如果我们不这么做，就不会有新的太阳，大地就会变得黑暗而寒冷。"

从那天起，铃木一郎不再担心了。

---

crash *v.* 碰撞；撞击   feed *v.* 供给；供应

He played happily in the trees. He knew there would always be light and heat as long as the villagers took coal and wood to the mountain.

他在树上开心地玩耍着。他知道只要村民们提供木头和煤炭给大山，就会有光明和热量。

How Glooskap Found Summer

Long ago, it grew very cold. Ice and snow covered the land.

Fires could not keep people warm, and corn could not grow.

Glooskap, the *leader* of the people, had to do something.

Glooskap traveled far to the north.

Everywhere he looked was cold and white with snow. He came to a house made of *solid* ice where a giant named Winter lived.

格卢斯卡普是如何找到夏天的

很久以前，天气非常寒冷，大地覆盖着冰雪。

借助火人们无法取暖，庄稼无法生长。

人们的领袖格卢斯卡普必须得做点什么了。

格卢斯卡普长途跋涉来到北方。

目光所及之处都很寒冷，到处是皑皑白雪。他来到一个叫作冬天的巨人的家里，他家房子是由坚固的冰块建造而成的。

leader *n.* 领导者；领袖   solid *adj.* 结实的；坚固的

Winter greeted Glooskap and invited him inside his house.

Winter began to tell stories of the time when he ruled the Earth. Soon Glooskap fell asleep under Winter's *spell*.

But Glooskap's *messenger*, Tatler, woke him.

"Wake up, Glooskap!" said the bird. "In the south, you will find a woman who can defeat Winter," said Tatler.

Glooskap traveled far to the south. He came to a land where it was warm and sunny.

Grass grew and flowers *bloomed* in the beautiful land.

Glooskap saw *spirits* dancing in a circle. At the center of the circle

---

冬天欢迎格卢斯卡普并邀请他到自己家里。

冬天开始讲他统治世界时期的故事。听着冬天的咒语，格卢斯卡普很快就睡着了。

但是格卢斯卡普的信使塔特勒叫醒了他。

鸟儿说："格卢斯卡普，醒醒！"塔特勒说："在南方有个女子可以打败冬天。"

格卢斯卡普长途跋涉来到南方。他来到一片温暖而阳光充足的土地。

在这片美丽的土地上，青草茂盛，鲜花盛开。

格卢斯卡普看到仙女们正围成圆圈跳舞。圆圈的中心是夏天，她棕色

---

spell *n.* 咒语　　　　　　　　　　　　messenger *n.* 送信人；信使
bloom *v.* 开花　　　　　　　　　　　　spirit *n.* 仙子；小精灵

was Summer. She wore a crown of flowers in her long brown hair.

Glooskap asked Summer to come north with him.

She followed him to Winter's house of ice. Winter invited them in and asked them to sit down. He began to tell stories again.

But Winter's spells could not *capture* Summer. She began to *chant* her own spell, and sweat ran down Winter's face.

"I am stronger than you," said Summer.

"You must leave this land and *thaw* your icy breath," she said.

Winter wept, and his tears became rivers of *melted* snow and ice.

的头发上戴着花冠。

格卢斯卡普让夏天和他一起回北方。

于是夏天跟随他来到冬天的冰屋。冬天邀请他们进屋并请他们坐下。然后他又开始讲故事了。

可是冬天的咒语对夏天不起作用。夏天也念起了咒语，于是冬天的脸上开始流汗了。

夏天说："我可比你厉害。"

她说："你必须离开这片土地，把冰雪融化。"

冬天哭泣了，他的泪水化作冰雪消融后的河流。庄稼生长了，鲜花再

---

capture *v.* 抓住；捕获　　　　　chant *v.* 反复地吟咏祷文；反复唱

thaw *v.* 解冰；融解　　　　　　melt *v.* （使）融化

The corn grew, and flowers bloomed again.

Summer told Winter, "You will have your own land in the north. It will always be winter there. You may come and visit other lands for part of the year. But in the spring, I will *drive* you out."

Since that day, Winter has ruled for part of the year. But every spring, Summer drives him away.

Sometimes it seems as if winter will never end. But Summer is stronger than Winter. Spring will always come.

次开放了。

夏天对冬天说："在北方你会有自己的土地，那里一直是冬天。一年中的部分时间里你可以去其他地方，但是春天时，我会把你驱赶走。"

从那天起，冬天开始统治一年的部分时间。但是每年春天，夏天就会把他驱赶走。

有时候似乎看起来冬天永远都不会过去，但是夏天比冬天厉害，春天总是会到来的。

drive *v.* 驱赶；赶走

3

The Tinosaur

Once the Earth was nothing more than one big *swamp*.

There were no people.

There were no roads and no houses.

The land was filled with *dinosaurs*, big and bigger—mostly bigger.

There were Supersaurs, Brachiosaurs, and the Brontosaurus.

All of them were big—very, very big.

The biggest of the big were the Ultrasaurs. They were so big that

微龙

从前地球不过是一片巨大的沼泽。

没有人。

没有道路和房屋。

陆地上到处都是大恐龙和更大的恐龙——多数是更大的恐龙。

有超龙、腕龙和雷龙。

他们都体型巨大——非常非常大。

在这些大家伙里超级龙最大。他们大到用"大"都不足以形容。他们

swamp　*n.*　沼泽

dinosaur　*n.*　恐龙

the word "big" is not big enough.

They lived in a big world.

Life was *fairly* easy for the big dinosaurs.

There were big plants to eat, and big lakes and rivers to drink from.

Life was good for the big dinosaurs.

As big as the big dinosaurs were, there were those that were small. In fact, they were smaller than small. They were *tiny*.

These little creatures were called Tinosaurs.

They would run here and there looking for food.

The best food was large *walnuts*. The walnuts were bigger than even they were.

生活在广阔的世界。

对于这些大恐龙来说，生活很舒适。

有巨大的植物可以吃，有大的湖泊和河流可以喝水。

这些大恐龙的生活很美好。

大恐龙有多大，相反，小恐龙就有多小。事实上，他们比"小"还要小。他们很微小。

这些小家伙叫作微龙。

他们跑来跑去寻找食物。

大核桃是最好的食物。核桃甚至比他们都大。

---

fairly *adv.* 一定地；相当地
walnut *n.* 核桃

tiny *adj.* 极小的；微小的

The Tinosaurs would *feast* on the nuts and eat and eat. While they ate, they would watch out for the Supersaurs.

For if a Tinosaur were stepped on by the Supersaur, it would be super *sore* indeed.

Things would have stayed this way for millions and millions of years, but something *scary* happened.

It all started one day. A Triceratops went *lumbering* by just as scared as he could be. "The ice is coming! The ice is coming!" he cried.

"Ice?" asked the Theropod. "Ice would be nice on a hot summer's day."

微龙们尽情享用着大核桃，不停地吃啊吃。他们吃的时候，还小心提防着超龙。

如果微龙被超龙踩着了，确实十分疼痛。

就这样数百万年过去了，然而发生了一件可怕的事。

有一天，三角龙惊慌失措地缓慢前行，他大声喊："冰来了！冰来了！"

兽脚恐龙问："冰？炎热的夏天有冰多好啊。"

---

feast *v.* 尽情享用   sore *adj.* 疼痛的

scary *adj.* 恐怖的；吓人的   lumber *v.* 缓慢吃力地移动

But ice wasn't nice. It wasn't nice at all. It was the coming of an ice age.

It wasn't long before it began to get cold and colder and colder.

The Theropods could see great *mounds* of ice—*glaciers*—*creeping* down from the mountains.

"We must move from here," said the Theropods. "We must escape to someplace warmer."

And with little thought or planning, they began moving away from the ice.

But the Tinosaurs were too small to escape. Their legs were too short and they could never run far enough.

"What are we to do?" one Tinosaur asked another. "If we stay

但是冰不好，一点也不好。冰河时期就要来了。

过了不久天气就变冷了，而且越来越冷。

兽脚恐龙看见了成堆的冰——冰川——从山上滑落。

兽脚恐龙说："我们必须离开这，逃到更暖和的地方。"

来不及思考和计划，他们就开始逃离。

但是微龙太小了，没办法逃走。他们的腿太短了，跑不了那么远。

一个微龙问另一个："我们该怎么办？如果我们待在这儿，会被冰埋上的！"

---

mound *n.* 一堆   glacier *n.* 冰川

creep *v.* 非常缓慢地行进；渐渐出现

here, we will be covered with ice!"

They thought and thought. Big plans for little creatures.

"We must find some place to stay warm," one finally said to another. "A place where we can hide from the ice," the other said in return.

"I have an idea!" said the first one. He quickly told them of his plan. "Follow me!"

With that, he searched about and found a large walnut shell.

The other Tinosaurs did the same.

They ate the meat inside until there were only hollow shells left.

Then, one by one, they each climbed inside a shell. They *twisted* and curled themselves inside and then pulled the top down tight.

他们不停地思考。小家伙们要想出大计划。

最后，一个微龙对另一个说："我们必须找到暖和的地方。另一个回答说："一个远离冰的地方。"

第一个微龙说："我有办法了！"他把自己的计划迅速地告诉了其他恐龙。"跟我来！"

于是，他寻找并找到了一个大核桃壳。其他的微龙也找到了大核桃壳。

他们吃光了里面的仁，只剩下了空壳。

然后，他们一个接一个地爬进壳里。他们扭动身体，让自己蜷缩在里面，接着把顶端盖紧。

---

twist v. 使弯曲；使扭曲

Safe and warm in the hard shells, they fell fast asleep. They slept as the Earth turned cold. Sadly, all the other dinosaurs became *extinct* during the ice age.

The Tinosaurs slept and slept, waiting for the ice to melt. And, in time, it did.

After the ice melted and the days became warm, all over the world, Tinosaurs crawled out of their walnut shells. But to this day, some Tinosaurs remain asleep in their shells.

If you are lucky, some day you may *crack* open a walnut shell and there find a Tinosaur, fast asleep.

坚硬的壳里既安全又温暖，他们很快就睡着了。在他们睡着的时候，地球变冷了。在冰河时期，令人伤心的是其他恐龙灭绝了。

微龙们一直在睡觉，直到冰融化了。他们醒得很是时候。

冰融化以后，天变暖和了，全世界的微龙从核桃壳里爬出来了。但是至今，仍然有还在核桃壳里睡觉的微龙。

幸运的话，有朝一日你用力敲碎一个核桃壳，会看见一个熟睡的微龙。

---

extinct *adj.* 已灭绝的；绝种的   crack *v.* 砸开；打碎

Go Away, Sun!

"Go away, Sun!" said Jackrabbit. "You're too bright, and I can't find any *shade* to rest in.

Sun's feelings were hurt. He moved west in the sky. As he moved above the *cottonwood* trees, he created shade in the grass below.

"Much better," said Jackrabbit. She *flattened* her ears against her

---

太阳，走开！

长耳大野兔说："太阳，走开！你太亮了，我都找不到树荫休息了。"

太阳很难过，他移动到了天空的西边。当他从棉白杨的上方经过的时候，在树下的草地上形成了树荫。

长耳大野兔说："这回好多了。"她把耳朵贴在后背上，躺下来休息。

---

shade *n.* 阴凉处；背阴   cottonwood *n.* 棉白杨
flatten *v.* 使紧贴；使贴着

back and lay down to rest.

"Go away, Sun!" said Rattlesnake. "Your strong rays have made this rock too hot to lie on."

Sun began to feel *gloomy*. He hid his face in the clouds and began to cry. Tears of sadness fell from the sky, cooling the desert floor.

" Much better," said Rattlesnake. He curled himself up in the sand and shook his *rattles* to warn others not to bother him.

"Go away, Sun!" said Roadrunner. "This desert is far too hot. All of the animals that I'd like to eat are hiding."

Sun was very sad because of Roadrunner's remark. He decided to hide behind the mountains. As he slowly began to sink, beautiful shadows appeared along the *horizon*. All of the desert animals came

---

响尾蛇说："太阳，走开！你的光线太强了，把石头烤得这么热，都没法在上面休息了。"

太阳觉得很沮丧，他把脸藏在云里哭泣。伤心的泪水从天空掉落，沙漠变得凉爽了。

响尾蛇说："这回好多了。"在沙子上他卷起身子，摇动着尾巴发出声音来警告其他动物不要打扰他。

走鹃说："太阳，走开！沙漠太热了，我要吃的动物都藏起来了。"

走鹃的话让太阳很伤心，他决定躲到大山后面去。他慢慢落下的时候，沿着地平线出现了漂亮的影子。沙漠里的动物都出来看他的影子。

---

gloomy *adj.* 忧郁的；沮丧的　　rattle *n.* （响尾蛇尾部的）角质环，响环
horizon *n.* 地平线

out to see them.

"Much better," said Roadrunner. She *dashed* after a small lizard that had come out to see the shadows.

"Go away, Sun!" said Kangaroo Rat.

"You're still shining on the tops of the mountains! I'm hungry, and I'd like to gather my food without you around."

Kangaroo Rat's cold words made Sun disappear over the horizon. As he went, he created a dusty rose and orange sunset.

"Much better," said Kangaroo Rat. She left her *burrow* in search of food.

Night fell, and the desert air and sand began to cool.

Jackrabbit fed on grasses while keeping a watch out for enemies.

走鹃说："这回好多了。"她快速追赶着一只出来看影子的小蜥蜴。

小更格卢鼠说："太阳，走开！"

"你还在山上照呢！我都饿了，我愿意在你不在的时候把食物收集到一起。"

听了小更格卢鼠冰冷的话语，太阳消失在地平线。在他离开的时候，形成了灰暗的玫瑰色和橙色的日落。

小更格卢鼠说："这回好多了。"她离开洞穴寻找食物去了。

夜晚到来了，沙漠中的空气和沙子开始变凉了。

长耳大野兔一边吃草，一边对敌人保持着警惕。响尾蛇在窝边寻找着

dash *v.* 急奔；猛冲   burrow *n.* （动物的）洞穴；地道

Rattlesnake stayed close to his den searching for small *rodents* to eat. Roadrunner dined on tasty lizards. Kangaroo Rat gathered seeds.

The animals noticed that it had been dark for quite some time. Sun had not appeared as usual. They began to wonder what had happened to him.

"Come back, Sun!" said Jackrabbit. "How am I supposed to rest in total darkness?"

"Come back, Sun!" said Rattlesnake. "How am I supposed to sun myself on the rocks?"

"Come back, Sun!" said Roadrunner. "How am I supposed to warm myself from this cool night air? I haven't had a chance to build

---

可以作为食物的小型啮齿动物。走鹃吃着美味的蜥蜴。小更格卢鼠把种子收集到一起。

动物们发现天黑已经很长时间了。太阳没有像平时一样出现，他们开始担心太阳出了什么事。

长耳大野兔说："太阳，回来呀！我怎么在一片漆黑之中休息啊？"

响尾蛇说："太阳，回来呀！我怎么在石头上晒太阳啊？"

走鹃说："太阳，回来呀！我怎么在这冰冷的夜晚的空气中取暖啊？我还没来得及用树枝垒窝呢。"

---

rodent *n.* 啮齿动物

my *nest* of *sticks*."

"Come back, Sun!" said Kangaroo Rat. "How am I supposed to dry the seeds that I've spent all night collecting?"

Sun brightened as he heard the animals asking him to return. Suddenly, he had a warm feeling inside.

The animals looked to the east and saw a faint glow in the sky. There, along the horizon, they saw a *radiant* Sun *peeking* up over the mountains.

小更格卢鼠说："太阳，回来呀！我怎么把整个晚上收集起来的种子晒干呢？"

听到动物们要求他回来，太阳高兴了起来。忽然之间心里觉得很温暖。

动物们望向东方，看到天空中微弱的红光。他们看到了沿着地平线，躲藏起来的太阳正在从山上升起，光芒四射。

---

nest *n.* 窝　　　　　　　　　　　　　stick *n.* 枝条；枯枝
radiant *adj.* 灿烂的；光芒四射的　　　peek *v.* 微露出；探出

26

5

The Disappearing Moon

The Scared Squirrel

Squirrel was scared.

He could not eat.

He could not sleep.

He could only worry.

"What is the matter, Squirrel?" asked Raccoon. "Why are you so worried?" "Haven't you noticed?" asked Squirrel. "The moon is

---

消失的月亮

惊慌的松鼠

松鼠很害怕。

他吃不下东西。

他睡不着觉。

他一直担心。

浣熊问："松鼠，你怎么了？为什么闷闷不乐的？"松鼠说："你还没注意到吗？月亮正在消失。趁现在还来得及，我们得多弄些食物来。"

---

squirrel *n.* 松鼠

disappearing. We need to get all the food we can now, before it is too late."

Deer and Raccoon looked up at the moon.

"The moon is not disappearing," said Raccoon.

"Yes, it is," said Squirrel. "It is smaller than it was last night. Just wait. Tomorrow, it will be even smaller."

The next night, the animals looked at the moon.

"Is the moon really getting smaller?" asked Deer.

"I don't know," said Raccoon.

But there was no question a few nights later.

The moon really was smaller.

"Squirrel is right," said Raccoon. "The moon is disappearing."

鹿和浣熊抬头看月亮。
浣熊说："月亮没消失啊。"
松鼠说："没错，但是它比昨天晚上小了。等到明天会更小的。"
第二天晚上，动物们看月亮。
鹿问："月亮真的变小了吗？"
浣熊说："不知道。"
毫无疑问，之后的几个晚上月亮确实变小了。
浣熊说："松鼠是对的，月亮正在消失。"

---

disappear *v.* 消失

"What is this I hear about the moon disappearing?" asked *Skunk*.

"Look!" Squirrel pointed up at the moon. "Only three-quarters of the moon was left now."

"It is disappearing," said Skunk.

The Wise Old Owl

A few nights passed and only half of the moon was left. The animals feared the moon would soon disappear.

After a week their fears came true.The moon disappeared. They all ran to wise old Owl to tell him that the moon had disappeared.

"You're all very *silly*," said Owl. "Gather around and I will teach you a lesson about the moon."

臭鼬问："我听说月亮正在消失，是吗？"

松鼠指着月亮说："看！现在月亮只剩下四分之三了。"

臭鼬说："它正在消失。"

博学的老猫头鹰

过了几个晚上，月亮只剩下一半了。动物们担心月亮很快就会消失。

一周以后，他们的担心成为了事实。月亮消失了。他们都跑着去找博学的老猫头鹰，告诉他月亮消失了。

猫头鹰说："你们都很糊涂啊。过来，我给你们上一堂课，讲讲月亮。"

---

skunk *n.* 臭鼬

silly *adj.* 愚蠢的；没头脑的

"There are two things you need to know about the moon," said Owl. "First, the moon does not shine on its own. The sun *lights up* the moon. Second, the moon does not sit still in the sky. It moves around Earth."

"Oh, yes," said Owl. "There is one more thing you need to know. The moon is like a ball."

"The sun can only light up one side of the moon. So when the moon moves around Earth, you see only the part of the side that the sun lights up."

Owl went on to say that sometimes you only see half of the

猫头鹰说:"关于月亮,你们需要知道两件事。第一,月亮本身不发光,是太阳照亮了月亮。第二,月亮不是在天上一动不动,它绕着地球转。"

猫头鹰说:"哦,对了,你们还需要知道一件事,月亮就像球一样。"

"太阳只能照亮月亮的一边。所以当月亮绕着地球转的时候,你们看到的只是太阳照亮那边的一部分。"

猫头鹰接着说有时你们只能看到照亮那部分月亮的一半,他说:"这

---

light up   (使)光亮;放光彩

lighted side. "This is called a half moon," he said.

"At other times you see all of the lighted side. This is called a full moon."

"And sometimes you do not see the lighted side at all. You see the dark side. This is called the *new moon*."

"But don't worry. The moon did not disappear," said Owl.

"Soon after a new moon, you will see a small part of the lighted side come back."

The other animals began to feel better after listening to Owl talk.

A few nights after Owl's lesson, the animals were out playing.

叫半月。"

"有时候你们看到的是照亮部分的全部，这叫做满月。"

"有时你们根本看不到照亮的那边，看到的是无光的一边。这叫作新月。"

猫头鹰说："但是不要担心，月亮不会消失的。新月之后不久，照亮那边的一小部分就会回来了。"

听了猫头鹰的话后，其他动物感觉好多了。

猫头鹰的课之后过了几晚，动物们出来玩。

---

new moon　新月

Squirrel looked up and saw a small *sliver* of the moon.

"Owl was right," Squirrel *yelled*. "The moon is coming back!"

The moon grew bigger each night. Soon there was a full moon again.

The animals had a full moon party!

松鼠抬头看见了小小的一条月亮。

松鼠大喊："猫头鹰说得对，月亮又回来了！"

每天晚上的月亮都比前一天的大。不久就又是一轮满月了。

动物们举行了一场满月晚会！

---

sliver *n.* 小块；薄片　　　　　　　　　　　　　　yell *v.* 叫喊；大喊

Migrating Geese

When the days get shorter, the geese fly south.

When the temperatures get colder, the geese fly south.

When the leaves fall from the trees, the geese fly south.

It is fall, and winter will soon arrive.

The land will be covered with snow and ice.

The geese fly south in groups called *flocks*.

迁徙的大雁

当白天变短的时候，大雁飞向南方。
当天气变冷的时候，大雁飞向南方。
当树叶从树上飘落的时候，大雁飞向南方。
秋天了，冬天很快就会到来。
大地将被冰雪覆盖。
大雁成群结队地飞向南方。

flock *n.* 群

They go to a warmer place. They take to the sky, and they get into *formations shaped* like the letter V.

They head for a warmer place. They are *migrating*.

Flying in a V-formation helps the geese to fly long distances. The V-formation makes it easier for the geese to move through the air.

They can cut through the air like a knife.

The goose in the front of the formation has to work the hardest. The geese take turns flying in the front.

When the goose in front gets tired, a goose from the back takes its place.

This is how geese in a flock work together.

Sometimes a goose in a flock gets injured and has to stay

他们飞往更温暖的地方。他们飞上天空，排成V字型。
他们飞往更温暖的地方。他们迁徙。
排成V字形有助于长距离飞行。V字形使大雁更容易穿过大气。
他们像刀一样穿过大气。
飞在前面的大雁必须承担最辛苦的工作。他们轮流飞在前面。
前面的大雁累了，队伍后面的大雁就会来接替。
这就是大雁群的工作方式。
有时群里的一只大雁受伤了，不得不待在队伍后面。会有一只大雁陪着它待在后面。

formation *n.* 编队；队形
migrate *v.* 迁徙
shaped *adj.* 具有(或呈)……形状的

behind. Another goose stays behind with the injured goose.

It stays until the injured goose gets better.

When the injured goose gets better, it continues to migrate.

The other goose that stayed behind migrates, too.

Geese are like a family. They take care of each other.

If one goose needs help or is in danger, other geese are there to help.

The migrating geese find a warmer place. They find a place where lakes and rivers are not *frozen*. They find a place where the land is not covered with snow. They find a place where there is plenty of food to eat.

They stay until the days in the north begin to get longer once again. They stay until the temperatures in the north get warmer once

---

这只大雁会一直陪着，直到受伤的大雁身体恢复。

等受伤的大雁身体恢复了，它会继续迁徙。

陪它待在后面的大雁也是一样。

大雁群就像一个家庭，他们彼此照顾。

如果有大雁需要帮助或是有危险，其他大雁都会来帮忙。

迁徙的大雁找到了更温暖的地方，那里的湖泊和河流不结冰，那里的大地没有白雪覆盖，那里有许多食物可以吃。

它们待在那儿直到北方的白天又一次开始变长。它们待在那儿直到北方的气温又一次变暖。它们待在那儿直到北方的树木又一次发芽、草又一

---

frozen *adj.* 冰封的；封冻的；结冰的

again. They stay until the trees in the north begin to leaf out and the grass begins to grow.

Once again it is time to migrate.

But this time the geese fly north. It is spring.

In the north, the snow and the ice have melted. Food is *plentiful*, and spring has arrived.

The geese *mate* and build a nest.

The female lays eggs. Soon there will be baby geese.

The baby geese have *hatched*. They are called *goslings*. Their parents will care for them and teach them to fly. Soon it will be time to migrate again.

次生长。

又到迁徙的时候了。

但是这次是飞向北方，因为春天来了。

在北方，冰雪消融，食物丰富，春天已经来了。

大雁们交配，筑巢。

母雁产蛋，雁宝宝很快就会出世了。

雁宝宝孵出来了，叫作 幼鹅。他们的父母会照顾他们、教他们飞。次迁徙的时间很快就又会到来了。

---

plentiful *adj.* 大量的；充足的
hatch *v.* 孵出；出壳

mate *v.* 交配
gosling *n.* 小鹅；幼鹅

Keb Needs a Home

The life of a hermit crab isn't so bad. They live near the *seashore*, and they *bask* in the warm sun. They bathe in the salty sea, and they play in the surf.

The views are great, too. Sunrises and sunsets can be pretty *spectacular*. And you can't beat the night sky with all its twinkling stars.

But for one hermit crab, life was not so great.

You see, Keb was a Hermit crab of spectacular proportions.

科比需要一个家

寄居蟹的生活没那么糟糕。他们住在海滨附近，在温暖的阳光下晒太阳。他们在咸咸的海水里游泳，在海浪中嬉戏。

景色也很棒，日出和日落相当壮观。还有你无法逃避挂满闪烁星星的夜空。

但是对于一只寄居蟹来说，生活并不如此美好。

你看，科比只是数量众多寄居蟹中的一员。

---

seashore *n.* 海岸；海滨   bask *v.* 晒太阳；取暖
spectacular *adj.* 壮观的；壮丽的

You might think that being the biggest crab on the seashore had its advantages. However, for Keb, the advantages were *few and far between*.

One of the biggest problems with being big was just that—being big. Being big made it easy for hungry gulls to spot Keb as they hung like kites in the *stiff* sea breeze.

But there was a bigger problem.

Keb could not find a home that was big enough for him.

Hermit crabs live in the *discarded* shells of snails. As a crab grows, it moves out of one shell and into a bigger one.

你也许认为作为海滨上最大的寄居蟹是有优势的。但是，对于科比来说，优势却少之又少。

大寄居蟹的最大问题之一是——大。大寄居蟹很大，饥饿的海鸥就像风筝一样在凛冽的海风中挂在天上，它们能轻易地发现科比。

还有更大的问题，科比找不到足够大的家。

寄居蟹住在废弃的螺蛳壳里。随着寄居蟹的不断生长，他从一个壳里搬出来，搬进一个更大的壳里。

---

few and far between　稀少；不常发生　　　　　　stiff　*adj.*　艰难的；激烈的
discard　*v.*　丢弃；抛弃

The trouble is that most snails are not very big.

Now, that is not a huge problem for most normal-sized crabs, but for Keb it was a problem of great *enormity*.

Keb walked sideways up and down the shore. He searched and searched for a shell big enough to use as his home.

He waited and waited, hoping that soon one day a large shell would wash up on shore.

While he waited to find a proper home, Keb lived in a large hole in a rock. Now, the hole was a fine home for most animals, but it was not a proper home for a hermit crab.

问题是大多数螺蛳都不是很大。

这对于大多数寄居蟹来说不是大问题，但是对于科比来说却是个很大的问题。

科比横着身子在海滨走来走去。他在寻找一个足够大的壳来作为自己的家。

他等啊等，希望很快有一天一个大的壳冲到岸上来。

在他等待着找到合适的家的这段时间，科比住在一个大石洞里。对于大多数动物来说，石洞是个不错的家；但是对于寄居蟹来说，这并不是合适的家。

enormity *n.* 巨大；严重性

Whenever Keb wanted to go out, he felt *naked*.

The other hermit crabs made fun of him, and the gulls *swooped* down to try to make him their dinner.

Keb always managed to escape the gulls, but the teasing from other crabs hurt *to the core* of his feelings.

To hide his nakedness, Keb tried everything.

First he gathered feathers he found along the shore and strung them together with old fishing line.

Then he *wrapped* them around his soft shell.

But the other crabs thought he looked silly.

"Look at Keb now," they said. "He thinks he's a bird. The next thing you know, he will try to fly."

无论何时科比想出去，他都感觉到赤裸裸的。

其他寄居蟹取笑他，海鸥猛扑过来试图把他当作晚餐。

科比总是设法逃脱，但是来自其他寄居蟹的嘲笑彻底伤了他的心。

科比尽一切努力来掩盖赤裸。

首先他沿着海岸收集羽毛，用旧鱼线捆扎起来。

然后把它们包在自己的软壳外边。

但是其他寄居蟹认为他看起来很愚蠢。

他们说："看看科比，他以为自己是只鸟。你知道的，下一步他会尝试着飞的。"

---

naked *adj.* 裸露的；不穿衣服的

to the core   十分；彻底地

swoop *v.* 向下猛冲；俯冲

wrap *v.* 包；裹

Keb's feelings were hurt even more.

He *threw off* the feathers and returned to his hole in the rock.

Next he gathered *seaweed* and wove it together to make a fine-looking suit.

But soon the seaweed began to *rot* and smell. The smell was so bad that not even Keb could stand it. So he threw away his seaweed suit and returned to his hole in the rock.

Peering out of his hole one morning, Keb noticed something strange had washed ashore.

He crawled out of the hole to take a closer look.

As he got closer he could see it was a boot. And it was a very fine boot.

科比的感情受到了更大的伤害。

他脱掉了羽毛，回到了石洞。

然后他收集海藻，并用海藻编制好看的套装。

但是海藻很快就腐烂发臭。气味非常难闻，以至于科比无法忍受。于是他丢掉了海藻装，回到了石洞。

一天早上，科比从石洞向外看，他看见一个奇怪的东西被冲到了岸上。

他从洞里爬出来，去看个仔细。

走近的时候，他看见那是只靴子，一只很好的靴子。

---

throw off　匆匆脱掉；拽下
rot　*v.* (使)腐烂；腐败变质

seaweed　*n.* 海草；海藻
peer　*v.* 仔细看；端详

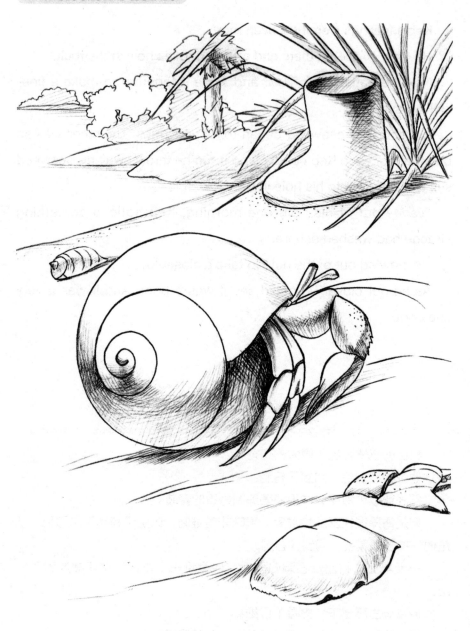

The boot was bright blue, which was Keb's favorite color in the world. He had always admired the blue *starfish* in the tide pools and he thought that blue crabs were the most handsome of all crabs. He had looked for a blue snail shell for a home when he was a smaller crab, but he had never found one.

Keb examined the boot more closely. It was made of rubber and would be perfect for stormy days when the cold wind and rain blew off the sea. And on the toe of the boot were two large eyes. "Ah-ha," thought Keb. "These eyes will surely *scare off* the swooping gulls."

And best of all, the boot was large. Keb looked inside and sized it up. The boot was definitely big enough for Keb's *enormous* body. He *crawled* into the boot. It was a perfect fit.

靴子是亮蓝色的，那是世界上科比最喜欢的颜色。他一直羡慕潮水坑里的蓝海星，他认为蓝色寄居蟹是所有的寄居蟹里最漂亮的。他小时候就开始寻找蓝色的螺蛳壳作为家，但是却没有找到。

科比走得更近，以便检查靴子。靴子是橡胶的，应对从海面吹来冷风和暴风雨天气会很不错的。靴子的头有两只大眼睛。科比想"啊哈，这眼睛一定会把袭击我的海鸥吓跑的。"

最重要的是靴子很大。科比朝靴子里看了看并估计了一下大小。很显然对于科比庞大的身躯来说，靴子足够大。他爬进了靴子，真的非常合适。

---

starfish *n.* 海星　　　　scare off 吓退；吓跑
enormous *adj.* 巨大的；庞大的　　crawl *v.* 爬行；匍匐行进

Keb *strutted* down the shore wearing his new home.

The gulls were frightened by the two large eyes looking up at them.

All the other crabs ooooed and aaaahed as Keb walked by.

They were *envious* of Keb's beautiful new home.

Keb was not only the biggest crab on the shore, he was also the most handsome.

The next week, Keb had an *open house*. All the other crabs came to see Keb's home, and they all brought him gifts.

Keb was no longer the *laughing stock* of all the crabs. He was the envy of the seashore.

科比背着新家在海滨大摇大摆地走。

两只大眼睛盯着海鸥看，把他们吓得要命。

科比走过的时候，其他所有的寄居蟹都发出"噢"、"啊"的声音。

他们羡慕科比的新家。

科比不仅是海滨最大的寄居蟹，也是最漂亮的。

过了一周，科比举行了家庭招待会。所有其他的寄居蟹带着礼物前来参观科比的家。

科比不再是其他寄居蟹的笑柄，大家都羡慕他。

---

strut *v.* 趾高气扬地走

open house 家庭招待会；开放参观日

envious *adj.* 羡慕的；嫉妒的

laughing stock 笑柄；笑料

8

The Sleeping Dog

Long ago, in the time before there were people, a dog was found sleeping in the middle of a dark forest. It was sleeping on its side with its legs *spread* in front of it.

It was happy. It was the first dog ever to live on the Earth. Most of the time, the dog just slept.

That the dog sleeping all day wasn't a problem. But it became a problem when a monkey saw it lying there. Now, the monkey was a nice enough animal, but it caused more than its share of trouble.

嗜睡的狗

很久以前，在有人类之前，黑森林当中有一条睡着的狗。它蜷着身子睡觉，腿向前伸着。

它很快乐。它是生活在地球上的第一只狗。大多数时间里它只是睡觉。

狗整天睡觉不是个问题，但是当猴子看见他躺着就成为问题了。猴子是不错的动物，但它造成了很多麻烦。

---

spread *v.* 伸开；伸展

The monkey jumped from a tree to the ground. It looked at the dog from the front and then from the back. The monkey couldn't *make head or tail of* this creature. So the monkey climbed into a tree and hung upside down to see if the dog looked different from that *angle*. The dog looked just the same upside down.

The monkey couldn't *figure out* what the dog was. Remember that this was the very first dog on Earth. No one had ever seen a dog before.

The monkey wanted to tell the other animals what it had found. Monkeys, as I'm sure you know, have big mouths.

Many animals came to see what the monkey had found.

"So," the monkey began, "this is the new creature I have found. Have any of you ever seen one before?"

　　猴子从树上跳到地上。它从前面看狗，然后又到后面看。对于这种动物它摸不着头脑。于是它爬到树上，倒挂着从那个角度看狗是否有什么不同。倒着看狗也是一样的。

　　猴子弄不明白狗是怎么回事。记住这可是地球上的第一只狗啊，之前谁也没见过狗。

　　猴子想告诉其他动物它的发现。我确信你们知道的，猴子有一张大嘴。

　　许多动物都赶来看猴子的发现。

　　猴子说："这是我发现的新动物。你们有谁以前见过？"

---

make head or tail of　　了解；弄清楚　　　　　　　　　　angle n. 角；角度
figure out　　弄懂；弄清楚

An elephant bent its head way down and looked at the dog. "Well," said the elephant, curling its *trunk* as it spoke, "it's not an elephant."

"Thanks a lot," said Monkey. "You aren't being very helpful."

Next in line was a gentle *okapi*.

It took a good look at the sleeping dog. In a voice the others could barely hear, the okapi said, "Sorry, I can't help you. It's not an okapi, and I'm sure it isn't a giraffe."

Now it was the *pangolin's* turn. Its body was covered with rough *scales*. The pangolin was very slow. If the pangolin had any thoughts about the dog, no one would hear them. The pangolin looked at the

---

大象低下头看了看狗，卷着鼻子说："它不是大象。"

猴子说："非常感谢。可是你说的没什么用。"

接下来是温和的霍加皮。它仔细看了看睡着的狗，用其他动物勉强能听到的声音小声说："对不起，我帮不了你。它不是霍加皮，我确定它也不是长颈鹿。"

现在轮到穿山甲了。它的身体覆盖着粗糙的鳞，行动迟缓。如果穿山甲对于狗有什么看法，没有谁能听见它说话。穿山甲看睡着的狗看了很久。然后它反复晃动身体，趴在地上，没说一句话就睡着了。

---

trunk *n.* 象鼻　　　　　　　　　　okapi *n.* 霍加皮（一种非洲鹿）
pangolin *n.* 穿山甲　　　　　　　scale *n.* 鳞

sleeping dog for a very long time. Then it *rocked back and forth*, settled to the ground, and fell asleep without saying a word.

The monkey asked every animal to take a turn. They each looked at the sleeping dog. Not one of them knew what it was or whose family it belonged to.

A tortoise was sitting quietly in a tree. No one was sure how it had gotten up there, but that is another story. The tortoise was very smart and was also very old. It knew what the dog was. In fact, it knew just about everything there was to know. "Have you given up?" the tortoise asked the monkey.

The monkey replied, "Yes, I think so. We cannot decide whose

猴子让每个动物都轮流看。动物们都看了睡着的狗，没有谁知道它是谁、属于哪个家族。

乌龟安静地坐在树上。谁都不知道它是如何爬上去的，但那是另一件事。乌龟非常聪明，年纪也很大了。它知道狗。实际上，它知道一切。乌龟问猴子："你死心了吗？"

猴子回答："是的，我是这么认为的。我们无法决定它是哪个家族的。"

---

rock *v.* 摇动

back and forth　反复来回

family this creature is from."

Tortoise replied, "You might want to call him 'Dog' unless you have a better name. If you ask me, and you didn't, 'Dog' is the perfect name."

Hearing its name spoken, the dog woke up. It was not happy to be awake. It saw all the other animals staring at it.

"Who was mean enough to wake me up?" the dog asked. It wasn't feeling very polite. The dog *bared its* big, *pointed* teeth and *growled*. It barked and barked. All the animals scattered. They were afraid that the dog wanted to eat them.

The tortoise was safe in its tree, since dogs can't climb trees.

乌龟回答说："你可以叫它'狗'，除非你有更好的名字。你问我的话，我没有更好的名字。'狗'是个完美的名字。"

听到叫自己的名字，狗醒了。它很不情愿醒过来。它看见其他所有动物都盯着它。

狗问到："谁这么卑鄙把我弄醒了？"它的语气很不客气，露出锋利的大牙咆哮着。动物们都散开了，它们害怕狗要吃它们。

乌龟在树上很安全，因为狗不会爬树。乌龟笑着说："你抓不到我。

---

bare one's teeth (凶恶地)龇牙咧嘴   pointed *adj.* 尖的；尖锐的
growl *v.* (动物，尤指狗)低声吼叫；咆哮

"You can't get me. But from now on, all the animals will run from you, and you will chase them," said the tortoise, laughing, as it *tucked* its head into its shell.

Even today, a dog will chase anything it sees, unless, of course, it is sleeping. Dogs still like to sleep, too.

That night Monkey sang a new song:

"So now we all know why you let a sleeping dog lie."

On that day, though, the animals had already made the mistake of waking up the sleeping dog. But a *lesson* was learned, and it has been *passed down* over time. Even today, it is best to let a sleeping dog lie.

但是从现在开始，所有动物都会逃离你，你会追逐它们。" 同时它把头缩进了龟壳里。

即使在今天，狗也会追逐它看到的任何东西，除非它睡着了。狗仍然喜欢睡觉。

那天晚上猴子唱了一首新歌：

"现在我们知道为什么你让睡着的狗躺着了。"

虽然那天动物们犯错吵醒了睡着的狗，但是却吸取了教训，并且随着时间的流逝流传了下来。甚至现在，（人们常常说）最好让睡着的狗躺着（勿自找麻烦）。

---

tuck v. 把……藏入；使隐藏　　　　　　　　　lesson n. 经验；教训

pass down　使世代相传；流传

Crows Share a Pie

One delightfully sunny day, a large crow flew over Mrs. Smith's house. Looking down, he *spotted* a big, freshly baked pie cooling on the *window sill*. Because pie was his favorite thing in the world, he swooped down for a closer look.

As the crow *glided* by, he could tell that nobody was home. He safely landed on the window sill and eyed the wonderful-smelling pie. The crow became especially excited to see that it was a cherry

---

乌鸦分享馅饼

在一个令人心情舒畅的大晴天，一只大乌鸦从史密斯夫人家上空飞过。他往下看的时候，发现窗台上晾着一个新烤的大馅饼。因为馅饼是他最喜欢的食物，所以他俯冲下去看个究竟。

他滑行的时候，发现房子里没有人。他安全地着陆在窗台上，看着香气扑鼻的馅饼。当他发现这是一个樱桃馅饼的时候，乌鸦变得格外兴奋。

---

spot *v.* 看见；发现
glide *v.* 滑行；掠过

window sill *n.* 窗台；窗沿

pie.

"Oh boy, delicious cherry pie. My favorite," he said. "And it's all mine."

Just as he was about to take his first bite, a second crow *flapped* down and landed on the window sill with a *thump*.

"That's a *mighty* big and tasty-looking pie," she *cawed*. "You don't intend to eat it all by yourself, do you?"

"Well, I was sure thinking I would," answered the first crow. "Since I found it first, it's all mine."

"Don't be so selfish," replied the second crow. "You can certainly see that there's enough pie for two hungry crows. Besides, you'll feel far better sharing the pie than you will getting a tummy ache from

---

他说："噢，美味的樱桃馅饼是我的最爱。都是我的了。"

就在他打算咬第一口的时候，第二只乌鸦拍打翅膀，重重地落在阳台上。

她说："那是个很大并且看起来可口的馅饼。你不是打算自己都吃掉，对吧？"

第一只乌鸦说："哦，我确信我会都吃掉的。从我发现它开始，就都是我的了。"

第二只乌鸦回答："别那么自私。你肯定知道馅饼足够两只饥饿的乌

---

flap *v.* 振(翅)；(翅膀)拍打
mighty *adj.* 巨大的；非凡的

thump *n.* 重击；碰撞
caw *v.* 鸦叫

eating the entire thing. So how about giving some of it to me?"

The first crow took a few moments to think.

"I suppose I could share it with you. After all, it is a very large pie. How do you *propose* we divide it?" he asked.

"Let's just split it down the middle," offered the second crow. "That way you get one half, and I get the other half. It's fair if we each get equal halves of the pie, isn't it?"

"I suppose so," said the first crow.

The crow *sliced* the pie in half. Just as he finished cutting, two more crows landed with a *flutter* of black wings. They stared at the pie with bright, *greedy* eyes.

鸦吃。此外，分享这个馅饼比你都吃下去后感到胃疼会感觉更好的。所以分一些给我怎么样？"

第一只乌鸦想了一会儿。

"我想我可以和你分享，毕竟这是一张很大的馅饼。你打算怎么分呢？"他问道。

第二只乌鸦提供了意见，"我们从中间分开。那样你拿一半，我拿另一半。如果我们两都拿相同的半个馅饼，很公平，不是吗？"

第一只乌鸦说："我想是这样。"

乌鸦把馅饼从中间切开。刚切好，又有两只乌鸦扇着黑翅膀着陆了。

---

propose *v.* 提议；建议
flutter *n.* 振动翅膀

slice *v.* 切；割
greedy *adj.* 贪婪的；渴望的

"How about offering some of that tasty-looking pie to us?" they begged.

The first and second crows *glanced* at each other, wondering whether or not they could bear to give away some of the pie. They finally agreed that sharing was a good thing, so they decided to split the pie with the other two crows.

"How do we cut up the pie now?" asked the first crow.

The second crow, being the smarter of the two, suggested dividing each of the halves down the middle.

"Cutting each half into two pieces will make four equal slices. Each of us will have one-fourth of the pie," she said.

他们用明亮而贪婪的眼睛盯着馅饼。

他们请求说：“把那个看起来很美味的馅饼分一些给我们怎么样？”

第一只乌鸦和第二只乌鸦互相看了一眼，想知道他们是否能忍受把部分馅饼分给其他乌鸦。最终，他们赞成分享是一件好事，所以他们决定把馅饼分给其他两只乌鸦。

第一只乌鸦问：“现在我们怎么切馅饼呢？”

第二只乌鸦，就是两只里较聪明的那只建议把半个馅饼再从中间分开。

她说：“把每半个馅饼再分成两份就有相同的四块了。我们每个人都吃四分之一。”

---

glance *v.* 瞥一眼；匆匆一看

"Brilliant idea," said the first crow, and he cut the two halves in half, making fourths. "There—we've got four equal pieces. Now everyone should be happy. Let's eat!"

But before the first four crows could take even one bite of pie, four more crows *sailed* down and *perched on* the ledge beside them. They stared hungrily at the pie.

"How about being generous and sharing that lovely pie with some poor, hungry crows?" they pleaded.

There was a bunch of *squawking* and cawing among the first four crows. But they, too, agreed that sharing was a good thing, and they decided to give a portion of the pie to the four other hungry crows.

"好主意",第一只乌鸦说,他把每半个馅饼从中间分开,变成四份。"我们有四份同样的馅饼了。每个人都该高兴了吧。我们吃吧!"

但是在这四只乌鸦还没咬一口的时候,又飞来了四只乌鸦,落在窗台上,站在他们旁边。他们饥饿地盯着馅饼。

他们恳求说:"慷慨地和一些可怜、饥饿的乌鸦分享那可爱的馅饼怎么样?"

起初的四只乌鸦大声地抗议。但是他们也赞同分享是件好事,于是决定把一部分馅饼分给其他四只饥饿的乌鸦。

---

sail *v.* 掠;飘
squawk *v.* 尖声高叫

perch on 栖息;停留

"Now what are we going to do to make sure everyone gets an equal piece?" asked the first crow.

The second crow declared, "No problem. We just make eight equal pieces by cutting each of the fourths in half. That will mean we each get one-eighth of the pie. That's the fairest way to do it, and everyone should be happy."

"Sounds good to us," shouted all the crows. "Now, let's hurry and eat our pieces of pie before we have to split them into even smaller *fractions*."

Each hungry crow *gobbled down* one-eighth of the pie, and then they all flew off in search of more.

第一只乌鸦问："怎么才能保证每个人得到的一样大呢？"

第二只乌鸦说："没问题。我们把四份馅饼从中间切开，就变成相等的八份了。这意味着我们每个人都可以得到馅饼的八分之一。这是最公平的方式，每个人都该高兴的。"

所有的乌鸦都喊："听起来不错。现在，让我们在把馅饼分成更小份之前赶快吃掉吧。"

每只饥饿的乌鸦都狼吞虎咽地吃掉了八分之一的馅饼，然后飞走去寻找更多的食物去了。

---

fraction n. 小部分；少量   gobble down   狼吞虎咽；贪婪地吃

Owen and the Tortoise

It was a hot, sunny day in Kenya, a country on the eastern coast of Africa. A young, one-year-old *hippo* named Owen followed his mother into the Sabaki River. The water felt good as it washed over Owen's warm skin.

Deep under the ocean, a long way from where Owen bathed, the earth began to shake. The shaking caused a *giant* wave, called a *tsunami*, to form. Hundreds of miles away, Owen was not aware of the giant wave.

欧文和乌龟

这是非洲东海岸国家肯尼亚炎热而晴朗的一天。一岁的小河马欧文跟妈妈来到佐佐木河。欧文觉得河水溅到热乎乎的皮肤上很舒服。

距离欧文洗澡很远的深海下面，地面开始晃动。晃动导致产生了巨大的海浪，我们称之为"海啸"。数百英里外的欧文并没有意识到。

---

hippo *n.* 河马
tsunami *n.* 海啸

giant *adj.* 巨大的

As the tsunami silently made its way toward the Kenyan shore, *carefree* Owen was having fun bathing in the river. Ships at sea slowly rose and fell as the giant wave passed harmlessly beneath them.

Finally, as the wave came near the Kenyan shore, something strange happened. Water near the shore was *sucked* into the ocean, creating a strong *current*. Rivers began to empty and flow back into the sea. It was as if someone had pulled a *plug* from the bottom of the ocean. The water in the Sabaki River suddenly rushed out to sea.

Owen, like all hippos, was a great swimmer. But the strong current was simply too swift. Owen felt himself being pulled away from his mother and going with the water out to sea. He was helpless, and there was little he could do.

当海啸悄无声息地逼近肯尼亚海滨的时候，无忧无虑的欧文正在河里洗澡呢。即将到达岸边的巨浪从海上的船舶下面经过，没有造成任何伤害，船只是缓慢地起伏着。

最终，海浪接近肯尼亚海滨的时候，奇怪的事情发生了。靠近海滨的水被吸进了大海，产生了强大的水流。全部河水倒流回大海里，就像有人拔掉了海底的塞子。佐佐木河里的水瞬间涌入了大海。

和其他河马一样，欧文也是个游泳好手。但是这强大的水流太快了，欧文感觉自己正在被水流从妈妈身边冲走，然后和河水一起涌向大海。他很无助，却又无可奈何。

---

carefree *adj.* 无忧无虑的；无牵挂的
current *n.* (海洋或江河的)水流；潮流

suck *v.* 吸引；使卷入
plug *n.* 塞子

Owen continued to struggle against the strong current, and he soon tired. He finally gave up. Soon he found himself surrounded by salty seawater. He had been pulled from the safety of the river into a strange and *vast* new place.

Owen *spat* and sputtered as he tried to stay afloat. The saltiness of the ocean burned his *nostrils*.

It seemed only a matter of time until Owen would slip beneath the water and drown. Then, as suddenly as he had been pulled into the ocean, he felt himself racing back toward land. The tsunami had a hold of him. The giant wave was taking him back toward shore.

As the wave neared shore, it seemed to grow bigger and bigger,

---

欧文在强大的水流中不断挣扎着，很快就筋疲力尽了。他最终放弃了挣扎。他很快发现周围都是咸咸的海水——他已经从安全的河流来到了一个陌生而广阔的新地方。

欧文换气、喷水，试图漂浮在水面上。海水的咸味弄得鼻子很痛。

看起来，沉到水下淹死只是时间问题。就像他被瞬间推进大海一样，他感觉自己正在快速退回岸边。他被海啸控制住了，巨大的海浪正把他带回岸边。

越靠近岸边，海浪似乎变得越来越大，好像要淹没小河马。然后在所

---

vast *adj.* 辽阔的
nostril *n.* 鼻孔

spit *v.* 吐

swallowing up the little hippo. Then, as all waves nearing shore do, the wave began to *crest*. A white *frothy* top *spilled over*, and the tsunami poured forward onto the shore.

Owen, caught up in the huge breaking wave, was tossed about like a *cork*. As the wave broke, it threw Owen onto the shore with a KAA-THUD!

The little hippo tumbled and rolled, bumping into the debris the rushing water had brought along with him. Owen was pushed farther inland.

Finally the wave ran out of energy, and its water spread thinly

---

有海浪靠近岸边的时候，形成了浪峰。有白色泡沫的浪尖倾泻而下，海啸向岸边涌动。

欧文被卷入了浪花中，像一个软木塞一样随意地被浪花抛上去，落下来。浪停了，砰的一声，欧文被扔到了岸上。

小河马翻滚着，撞到了和他一起被海水冲上岸的残骸。欧文被冲到了更远的内陆。

最终海浪耗尽了能量，蔓延到地面的水只有薄薄的一层。躺在地上的

---

crest *v.* 到达浪峰；达到顶点
spill over 溢出；漫出

frothy *adj.* 有泡沫的；起泡沫的
cork *n.* 木栓；软木塞

over the land. Owen lay *bruised* and tired, far from the Sabaki River and his mother.

It was not long until a wildlife *ranger*, who was checking the damage the tsunami had caused, came across the little hippo. He was surprised to see a hippo so near the ocean's shore. He knew that hippos lived inland along the banks of rivers.

The ranger called for help, and Owen was transported to a wildlife park. Owen began to recover and gain strength, but Owen missed his mother.

Owen spotted a large, gray 100-year-old tortoise named Mzee. The tortoise was similar in color to Owen's mother.

欧文鼻青脸肿，疲惫不堪，距离佐佐木河和妈妈是那么遥远。

过了不久，一位检查海啸损毁情况的野生动物管理员发现了小河马。小河马离海岸这么近令他很吃惊，他知道河马住在内陆河的岸边。

野生动物管理员发出求救，欧文被运送到了野生动物公园。欧文开始恢复健康，积聚力量，但是他想妈妈了。

欧文发现了一只灰色的大海龟阿木积，他有一百岁了。他的肤色和欧文的妈妈很相似。

欧文迅速地靠近了阿木积。这只老乌龟似乎并不介意欧文在他旁边睡

---

bruise *v.* 撞伤；擦伤　　　　　　　　ranger *n.* 公园管理员；护林人

Owen was immediately drawn to Mzee. The old tortoise didn't seem to mind having Owen *cuddle up* to him or follow him around.

Owen and Mzee now eat, swim, and sleep together. Wherever Mzee goes Owen is at his side. Owen even tries to protect Mzee when someone comes near. It is just what he would do if Mzee really were his mother.

Owen was very lucky to survive the tsunami. And he was luckier to find a new mom, even if it was an old tortoise.

觉或者到处跟着他。

现在，欧文和阿木积一起吃东西，一起游泳，一起睡觉。无论阿木积去哪，欧文都跟在他身边。甚至在有人接近的时候，欧文试图保护阿木积，就像阿木积是他真正的妈妈一样。

能从海啸中幸存欧文很幸运，更幸运的是他有了新妈妈，虽然它只是一只老乌龟。

---

cuddle up　　紧靠……而坐(或躺)；依偎

A Late Night Chat with a Parakeet

My name is Hattie MacGruder. I am queen and absolute leader of my third-grade class, and I have a *parakeet*!

He's not one of those little silly singing birds, but a real talking parakeet.

He talks like there's no tomorrow. He talks about the weather and my friends and the silly seeds he has to eat.

He would much rather eat *chili* cheese fries, and he loves Britney

---

在深夜与长尾鹦鹉聊天

我叫哈蒂·麦格鲁德。我是三年级的女王和绝对领袖,我有一只长尾鹦鹉。

他不是又小又笨的鸣禽,他是真正会说话的长尾鹦鹉。

他拼命地说话。他说天气,说我的朋友,说他必须吃的傻乎乎的种子。

他宁愿吃红辣椒芝士薯条,他爱流行舞曲天后小甜甜。

---

parakeet n. 长尾鹦鹉

chili n. 辣椒

Spears.

I am telling the truth.

There are others who are not telling the truth.

Sybil and Sarah are liars and *fibbers* and tellers of untruth.

They said that there never was a talking parakeet. They said the parakeet never even tasted a chili cheese fry. Mostly they said that parakeets don't talk. They said that I'd made it all up. That's why they are liars and fibbers and tellers of untruth. Because there really was what I said there was—there always is and . . .

. . . plus, I have absolute proof about the talking parakeet and all the other things that happened to me.

The proof is in my diary. I'm going to let you read it exactly as I

我说的都是实话。

有些人不说实话。

西比尔和莎拉就是说谎的人，他们不说实话。

他们说根本没有会说话的长尾鹦鹉，长尾鹦鹉不吃红辣椒芝士薯条。他们说长尾鹦鹉不说话，都是我自己编造的。这就是他们说谎，不说实话的原因。因为实际上我说的——总是……

……加上我已经验证了这只说话的长尾鹦鹉和其他发生在我身上的事。

证据在我的日记里。我会让你正确地理解我记录的这只说话的长尾鹦

---

fibber *n.* 骗子；说谎的人

wrote it when the parakeet talked. That way, you can read, first hand, the truth about this matter.

Special Note:

I am only going to let you read the parts of my diary that are about the parakeet. You won't get to read the stuff about me getting *grounded* for *sassing* my teacher—which I didn't do. I *swear* somebody was playing tricks on me. Mom was so mad that she had to see my teacher. She wouldn't even let me buy the new Britney Spears CD I had been saving up for.

Mostly, you won't get to read anything about Sybil, Sarah, and me going to the movies on Sunday. We saw Libby Thompson,

---

鹉。这样，你就可以直接了解事情的真相。

特别说明：

我只是想让你阅读我日记中关于长尾鹦鹉的部分。你不会读到我因为和老师顶嘴而被禁足——我以前也没那么做过——的内容。我发誓有人捉弄我。妈妈知道老师要见她，很生气。我攒钱打算买的小甜甜的新CD，她甚至都不让我买。

你读不到关于西比尔，莎拉和我计划周日去看电影的任何内容。我们看见利比·汤普森了，她不是自己一个人坐着。她和土包子戴维·布鲁斯特坐在一起，有人认为他和我是朋友。但是他一定忘了周四午饭后我们的

---

ground *v.* 罚(儿童)不准出门   sass *v.* 粗鲁地说话；出言不逊
swear *v.* 郑重承诺；发誓

and she was not sitting alone. She was sitting with the *geek* of all geeks, Davey Brewster, who was supposed to be my friend. But he must have forgotten about our little talk after lunch on Thursday. Libby must have made him go with her—*blackmail* or something. And I am not going to let you read the part where Davey Brewster got her a soda. Or when he gave her the *gumball* that fell on the icky movie theater floor. She ate it! I hope she doesn't get a *fatal* disease or anything.

The Proof:

Diary, Day 117

It was kind of a sad day. My mom's aunt (my great-aunt) died. I didn't know her that well, but I was sad for my mom. I didn't go to the funeral, but my mom and dad did.

谈话。一定是利比让他跟着她——勒索或是做其他什么事。我不想让你们读戴维·布鲁斯特在哪给她买的汽水这部分。或者是他什么时候给她掉在影院令人作呕的地板上的口香糖这部分，而且她竟然吃了！我希望她别得绝症或是其他什么病。

证据：

日记，第117天

有点难过的一天。妈妈的姨妈（我的姑姥姥）去世了。我不是很了解她，但是我因为母亲而难过。我没去参加葬礼，父母去参加了。

---

geek *n.* 土包子
gumball *n.* 球形口香糖

blackmail *n.* 勒索；敲诈
fatal *adj.* 致命的；灾难性的

Then they went over to my great-aunt's house and everybody was sad together.

I spent the day at Sarah's house. Sybil came over, and we played cards, watched TV, and talked about Davey Brewster. He is so pop. He and I are special buds. We talked about it after lunch on the playground Thursday and decided that it was cool. He said he liked me better than any girl in the third grade. I like him better than any boy in the whole world. Well, except for Debbie Phillips's older brother, who I am going to marry when I retire from my career.

Anyway, I was supposed to spend the night at Sarah's, but my mom wanted me to come home.

She was in a much better mood when I got there. She didn't seem sad at

---

然后他们去了姑姥姥家，大家都很难过。

白天我呆在莎拉家。西比尔也来了，我们一起打牌，看电视，谈论戴维·布鲁斯特：他是如此受欢迎。他和我都与众不同。周四午饭后我们在操场上谈论了这事，并且觉得很酷。他说他喜欢我胜过其他三年级的任何女孩。我喜欢他胜过整个世界的任何男孩。当然，除了黛比·菲利普斯的哥哥，我打算退休后嫁给他。

总之，我想在莎拉家过夜，但是妈妈让我回家。

我回家的时候，她心情好了很多，看起来一点也不难过了。实际上，她相当高兴。她说在我的房间里有个惊喜正等着我呢。我确信是她不让我

---

bud n. 朋友；伙伴　　　　　　　　　　　mood n. 情绪；心情

all. In fact, she was pretty happy. She said there was a surprise waiting for me in my room. I thought for sure it was going to be the Britney Spears CD that she wouldn't let me get. It wasn't…

The surprise was a parakeet'my great-aunt's parakeet' which my great-aunt's husband (my great-uncle) had given to my mother. Mom said the parakeet was very special because it had belonged to my great-aunt. She said she knew I would take good care of it.

The parakeet seems to be happy in my room. I **whistled** *at it, and it whistled back. Wow, can it whistle and* **chirp** *and sing. It whistles really loudly. It won't knock it off! I hope that silly bird doesn't keep me awake all night!*

I've got to go to sleep now. I'll write longer later!

买的小甜甜的CD，但是不是……

  惊喜是一只长尾鹦鹉——姑姥姥的长尾鹦鹉——姑姥姥的丈夫（姑姥爷）送给妈妈的。妈妈说这只鹦鹉很特别，因为姑姥爷养了它很长时间。她说她知道我会照顾好鹦鹉的。

  长尾鹦鹉看起来在我的房间里很快乐。我冲它吹口哨，它也冲我吹口哨。哇！它会吹口哨，会叽喳叫，还会唱歌。它吹口哨声音很大，而且不停地吹。我希望这只愚蠢的鸟不要让我整晚睡不着觉！

  现在我得睡觉了。以后我会继续写的。

---

whistle   *v.* 吹口哨   chirp   *v.* 吱喳叫；唧唧叫

Diary, Day 117 (later)

What a night!

I tried to fall asleep, but that silly parakeet kept being happy' chirping, whistling, and making clicking sounds. When the cat started meowing, I just let her get up on the bed. I thought that maybe the bird was lonely. I turned on my light and looked at it. Actually, I told it to **shut up***. But it just sat on its little wooden* **swing** *and looked at me, whistling and chirping and making noises.*

I opened the cage door, reached in, and grabbed it. It stopped singing and didn't even flutter. My great-aunt must have taken it out of the cage a lot.

I climbed back into bed and set it down on my **pillow***. It kind of* **hopped** *around and then . . .*

. . . it talked.

日记 第117天（后来）

这个晚上太糟糕了！

我试图睡觉，但是那只长尾鹦鹉始终很高兴——它叽喳地叫，吹口哨，发出咔嚓的声音。猫开始喵喵叫的时候，我在床上把它叫醒。我想这鸟有可能感到孤独，我打开了灯看着它。事实上，我告诉它闭嘴。但是它站在小小的木质秋千上看着我，吹口哨，叽喳地叫，发出噪音。

我打开了笼子门，手伸了进去抓住了它。它不再唱歌了，甚至连翅膀都没有扇动。姑姥姥肯定经常把它拿到笼子外边。

我爬回床上，把它放在枕头上。它轻轻地跳来跳去，然后……

---

shut up   使某人住口；让某人闭嘴   swing *n.* 秋千

pillow *n.* 枕头   hop *v.* 跳行

I mean, he talked.

He said my great—aunt called him Freddie, but he much preferred Fred.

*I couldn't believe it! Fred was speaking just as clearly as you or I. "Well, my dear friend, Hattie," he said, "What do you want to do? Play cards? You do play Spite and Malice, don't you? Or maybe we could read a **teen magazine** or listen to some music. You do have the new Britney Spears CD, don't you?"*

*He talked on and on and on. He even **pooped** on my pillow, but I didn't care.*

With Fred still talking, I fell asleep.

*As I **drifted off**, he babbled on about flying south with the ducks for the*

……它说话了。

我是说，他说话了。

它说姑姥姥叫它弗雷迪，但是它更喜欢昵称。

我简直不敢相信！弗雷迪像你和我一样清晰地说话。它说："我亲爱的朋友哈蒂，你想做什么？打牌？你玩Spite and Malice（一种网游），对吧？也许我们还可以读青少年杂志，或者听音乐。你有小甜甜的新CD，对吧？

它不停地说。它甚至在我枕头上排便，但是我不介意。

在弗雷迪的喋喋不休中，我睡着了。

---

teen *adj.* 十几岁的；青少年的

poop *v.* 拉屎；大便

magazine *n.* 杂志；期刊

drift off 入睡；睡着

*winter or something. He thought the life of a **gypsy** duck was the life for him.*

Now, for the bad news. When I woke up, he was gone!

I don't know where he went. The cage was still there, but it was empty. My cat was asleep on the bed, just like she always is. The only things moving in the room were the curtains tossing in a light breeze that blew through the open window. There were some feathers on the floor fluttering with the breeze. But other than that, Fred was gone.

Mom was very upset. I tried to tell her that Fred had been talking about traveling with the ducks. Maybe he slipped out, met up with a big old group of wild ducks, and headed south. I told her he would probably come back in the spring. I'll bet that's what happened.

在我迷迷糊糊的时候，它不停地唠叨着和鸭子飞到南方过冬的事。它认为它的生活和吉卜赛鸭子的生活一样。

坏消息来了：我醒来的时候，它不见了！

我不知道它去哪了。笼子还在，但是空着。猫还在床上睡着，和往常一样。房间里唯一在动的东西是被窗外吹进来的微风晃动的窗帘。在微风吹拂下，地板上若干羽毛在飘动。但是除此之外，弗雷迪不见了。

妈妈感到很心烦。我试着告诉她弗雷迪说它和鸭子一起旅行过。也许它溜出去，遇到一大群野鸭子，然后飞到南方去了。我告诉她也许到了春

---

gypsy *n.* 吉普赛人

*Nothing was going to get me off the hook because Mom was really mad. She gave me the "**responsibility**" talk. I cried like I always do.*

I am grounded for today, but Sarah and Sybil still got to come over.

I wish they hadn't.

I told them all about the talking parakeet. I told them he even wanted to play cards, and he loved Britney Spears.

*I am so mad at Sarah and Sybil. They said I'd made everything up about Fred. They said the parakeet was probably in **heaven**. They even said they thought the cat ate him.*

They are liars and fibbers and tellers of untruth.

天它就回来了。我相信是这样的。

我摆脱不了困境因为妈妈真的生气了。她和我谈论了"责任",我像往常那样哭了。

我打算今天不出去的,可是莎拉和西比尔来我家了。

我多么希望她们没来啊。

我告诉她们关于说话的长尾鹦鹉的所有事。我告诉她们它甚至要打牌,喜欢小甜甜。

我对莎拉和西比尔很恼火。她们说关于费雷迪的一切都是我编造的。她们说长尾鹦鹉可能已经死了。她们甚至说她们认为猫吃了长尾鹦鹉。

---

responsibility *n.* 责任

heaven *n.* 天堂;天国

My diary proves it!

I hate them.

Mom felt bad about what happened and said I could go to the movies with Sarah and Sybil tomorrow. I called Davey Brewster to see if he could go, too. He said he had to go to church. We're going to the matinee. It's going to be a lot of fun.

Love,

Hattie MacGruder

她们说谎，不说实话。

我的日记可以证明！

我讨厌她们。

妈妈为发生的事感到难过，她说我明天可以和莎拉西、比尔去看电影。我给戴维·布鲁斯特打电话，问他是否能一起去，他说他必须去做礼拜。我们打算去看白天场，会很有趣的。

爱你的，

哈蒂·麦格鲁德

matinee *n.* （戏剧、电影的）午后场；日场

The Little Fir Tree

A Young Tree

The young, pencil-thin *fir* tree stood admiring his neighbors. The tall *oak* made him want to be taller and grander. The other *evergreen* trees seemed to laugh at his being so small.

He watched, year after year, as trees bigger than he were taken away each winter. He was sure that wherever they were, it was a *magical* place.

小冷杉树

一棵小树

这棵小的、像铅笔一样细的冷杉直立着，羡慕着它周围的树。那棵高高的橡树让它想要长得更高一些、更宏伟一些。其他的常青树好像在嘲笑他太小了。

他每年都看到这一切，比他长得大的树每年冬天都被带走了。他肯定，无论他们在哪里，那一定是一个神秘的地方。

---

fir *n.* 冷杉
evergreen *adj.* 常青树；常绿树

oak *n.* 橡树
magical *adj.* 有魔力的；奇妙的

It seemed that each tree taken away was special. The little fir tree's greatest hope was that he could be special, too.

He just knew there was more to life than birds' *bothersome flitting* through his branches, the sun's overly bright rays shining on the meadow, and the moon's *waxing* and *waning* each month.

Every year, when the snow came and the oak tree had no leaves, the fir tree watched as happy people chose special trees.

A bird told the fir tree a wonderful tale of seeing evergreens in warm homes, dressed in finery. The people would laugh and sing around the tree.

The fir tree thought this was the grandest sight. He imagined it every day as more and more seasons passed, and he grew taller

---

看起来每棵被带走的树都是特别的。小冷杉的最大愿望就是自己也会是特别的。

他知道,生活不只是烦人的鸟儿们在树间掠过,非常明亮的阳光照在草场上和月亮每个月的盈亏。

每年下雪的时候,橡树上不再有叶子了,冷杉看着快乐的人们选定特别的树。

一只鸟儿讲给冷杉一个迷人的故事,它看到在一个温暖的家里有长青植物,穿着华丽。人们围着这棵树欢笑、唱歌。

冷杉认为这是一个最宏伟的场面,随着季节的更替,他每天都在幻想

---

bothersome *adj.* 恼人的;烦人的

wax *v.* 盛衰;阴晴圆缺

flit *v.* 掠过

wane *v.* (月)缺;亏

still.

A Winter Adventure

The fir tree was sure this would be the year he was chosen. His branches *trembled* as he waited. The snow came, and then the happy people came. Group by group they chose evergreens from the forest. As he trembled, the snow fell from his branches.

As the sun nearly *faded away*, a group of laughing people gathered at his *trunk*.

He tried not to tremble too much. He didn't want to drop snow on them. He wanted them to think he was the grandest tree in the forest.

着此事，他也不断地长高。

冬天的一个历险

冷杉确定今年该是自己被选中的时候了，他在等的时候，枝叶都在颤抖。天下雪了，然后快乐的人们来了。他们一群群地从森林中选出常青树。他在颤抖着，雪从他的枝叶上落下来。

太阳的光线几乎消失了，一群笑着的人聚集在他的树干周围。

他努力让自己不发抖，他不想让雪从自己的身上掉下来，他想让这些人认为他是树林中最宏伟的树。

---

tremble *v.* 颤抖；哆嗦　　　　　　　　　　fade away　逐渐消失
trunk *n.* 树干

At last, they took out an *axe* and chopped him down. The happy people had taken the fir tree from his roots. The fir tree's trembling didn't stop as they *strapped* him to a shiny, red car that moved like the wind.

A short while later, the fir tree was carried into a warm home. They stood him upright in some kind of stand. The happy people tightened screws around his trunk. They talked about his fir needles falling all over the floor. Hearing this, the fir tree vowed to stop trembling. He didn't want to shake off his needles because the happy people might not want him anymore.

Later that night, many boxes were taken down from closets. First, they placed shiny bulbs in every color of the rainbow in a string

---

最后，他们拿出斧子，把他砍倒了。快乐的人们把冷杉从他的根部取了下来。在人们把他拖进一辆闪亮的红车中系好，冷杉的颤抖并没有停下来，这辆车跑起来像一阵风一样。

过了一小会儿，冷杉被带到一间温暖的房子里，他们把他放在一个类似于架子的东西上。快乐的人们绕着他的树干拧紧了螺丝。他们在谈论着他落在地上的细细松针。听到这些，冷杉发誓自己不再颤抖，他不想抖掉他的松针，这样快乐的人们就不再会要他了。

后来的那天晚上，人们从柜橱里取出很多的盒子。首先，人们把一串串闪着各种颜色的小球绕在他的周围，这些小球闪着光，朝冷杉眨着眼

---

axe *n.* 斧子　　　　　　　　　　strap *v.* 用带子系(或捆、扎、扣)好

around him. The bulbs twinkled and winked at the fir tree. This made him glow inside and out.

Next, the children placed *ornaments* of wood upon his *boughs*, while the adults placed those of glass. Strings of popcorn, cranberries, and *sprigs* of holly followed.

The fir tree couldn't help but tremble just a bit. He had never been so proud.

His deepest center warmed as candy canes and gingerbread men were hung from his branches. A bright, silver star at his top added the final touch.

The family—he could tell they were a family now—gathered around him. They told stories and sang songs well into the night.

睛。这让他从里到外地闪着光。

接下来，孩子们把木制的装饰物摆在他的树枝上，大人们摆上一些玻璃的装饰。接下来的是一串串的爆米花、越橘和枸骨枝。

冷杉控制不住地颤抖着，他从没有这么自豪过。

他的内心更加温暖，因为给在他的树枝上挂上了拐杖糖和姜饼人，明亮的银星挂在他的顶部，真是锦上添花。

全家人，他现在能确认这是一家人，都围在他的周围，他们讲故事，唱歌，一直到深夜。

---

ornament *n.* 装饰品

bough *n.* 大树枝

sprig *n.* (烹饪或装饰用)带叶小枝

Soon, the adults said good night to the children. Then they brought out paper of *shimmering* reds, golds, and greens. The fir tree watched as they brought out toys and clothes and wrapped each in paper before tying on a *bow*. They placed the wrapped packages under his boughs. The fir tree would protect them through the night.

He thought and thought about all that had happened. The fir tree went over each detail since he had left his forest home. He could not wait to tell the birds, the other trees, and all of the forest what had happened on this night.

Soon, he drifted off to sleep.

很快，大人们跟孩子说晚安了，然后他们拿出闪光发亮的红色、金黄色和绿色的纸，冷杉看到他们拿出玩具、衣服，把它们一个个包起来，然后系好蝴蝶结。他们把这些包好的盒子放在他的树枝下面。冷杉会整晚保护好这些东西。

他想呀想着所发生的一切，冷杉回忆着自他离开森林的家以后发生的所有细节。他已经等不及想要告诉森林里的鸟儿们和树们这个晚上发生的一切。

很快，他渐渐地进入了梦乡。

---

shimmer *v.* 发出微弱的闪光；闪烁　　　　　　　　　bow *n.* 蝴蝶结

The next morning, everyone in the house woke up early. The children reached for the packages. He felt so good and warm inside when they were gathered around his branches.

The fir tree trembled with excitement. He was not scared this time.

The adults talked and laughed as the children *marveled* over their gifts. They kept mentioning Santa Claus. This Santa sounded so *grand* to the fir tree that he wished he had met Santa during the night.

Soon the children tore open their gifts and scattered colorful paper about the room. They ran happily around the house playing

---

第二天早晨，每个人起得很早，孩子们伸手取这些包裹。当他们聚到他的周围时，他的内心感到很好、很温暖。

冷杉激动得发抖了，这回没有害怕。

在孩子们惊喜地看着自己的礼物时，大人们说着话，笑着。他们不时地提起圣诞老人，冷杉觉得这个老人非常了不起，他都希望自己在晚上能见到这个老人。

很快孩子们撕开各自的礼物，把撕碎的彩纸扔了一地，他们在屋内快乐地跑着，玩着他们的新玩具。大人们在冷杉旁的沙发上喝着热巧克力，

---

marvel *v.* 感到惊奇；大为赞叹　　　　　　grand *adj.* 了不起的；出色的

with their new toys. The adults drank hot chocolate on the couch near the fir tree. They stayed close to the fir tree throughout the day, and into the night.

A Lonely Feeling

The fir tree awoke the next morning as the family gathered coats, *mittens*, and hats. He wondered if they would take him along too. After a short time, they were gone.

The fir tree spent most of the day in the lonely quiet. Then, when the family came home, he was so excited. They rushed past him to play games around the kitchen table. Hours later, the fir tree heard them say good night.

He spent many days watching the family hurry past him to do this

---

整个白天到深夜他们都待在冷杉的旁边。

　　一种孤独的感觉

　　冷杉第二天早上醒来时，家里的人已经穿上外衣、戴上手套和帽子。他在想能不能也带上他。不大一会儿，他们都走了。

　　冷杉这一天是在孤独的安静中度过的。后来全家人回来了，他非常高兴。他们从他的身边跑过去，在餐桌的周围玩玩具。几个小时以后，冷杉听到他们说晚安了。

　　好多天以来，冷杉看到全家人从他的身旁匆匆而过，做这个做那个。

---

mitten *n.* 连指手套

and that. The fir tree began to wonder if they remembered he was there at all. Twelve days passed with the fir tree feeling lonely and ignored.

On the twelfth morning, the happy family took off his *glimmering* lights, glass ornaments, and the wooden ones, too.

They took him outside. He felt a *gust* of cold air, and he trembled.

They leaned him against a fence and left him there. It was dark and cold outside. He was lonely. He *hummed* quietly to himself, and talked to the moon. He remembered the *tunes* that the family had sung on the night Santa came.

Over many months, the fir tree felt the air around him grow warmer. He longed to see his forest home again, to talk to the birds,

---

冷杉开始想他们是不是记得他的存在。冷杉感觉到孤独和被忽视已经有十二天了。

第十二天早晨，快乐的家庭取下了发光的小灯、玻璃装饰物和木制的装饰物。

他们把他带到外面，他感到一阵冷风，他颤抖了一下。

他们把他斜靠在篱笆上，就把他放在那里了。外面是黑暗的，也很冷。他很孤独。他对自己哼唱着，他和月亮讲话，他记起了圣诞老人来的那个晚上全家人唱的曲调。

几个月过去了，冷杉感觉到周围的空气暖和了很多，他想再回到他的

---

glimmer *v.* 隐约地闪烁；发出微弱的闪光　　　　gust *n.* 一阵强风；一阵狂风

hum *v.* 哼(曲子)　　　　　　　　　　　　　tune *n.* 曲调；曲子

but most especially, he wanted to be *decked* in twinkling lights and shining ornaments. He wanted to tell the oaks in the forest about what he had seen. He wanted to tell the other evergreens about being chosen by a family, and about the two most *glorious* days of his life.

Spring is Here

One day, the fir tree felt his needles and branches *tickled* by a spring rain. The fir tree almost laughed with delight. Above him, the sun shone brightly and the air smelled of earth. The birds chirped in nearby trees.

One of the happy people *furrowed* the dirt near him to plant a

---

森林的家，去和鸟儿们说话，但最特别的是想被用闪光的灯和亮闪的装饰物装点起来。他想告诉森林里的橡树他看到的一切，他想告诉其他常青植物，被一个家庭挑选上了，还有他两天非常光彩的生活。

春天在这里

一天，冷杉感觉到他的松针被春天的雨水弄得痒痒的。冷杉高兴得笑出声来。在他的头上，阳光很明亮，空气中散发着泥土的味道，鸟儿们在附近的树上鸣叫。

快乐人们中的一个，在他附近的土地上翻土，在花园中种植物，这是

---

deck *v.* 装饰；布置；打扮
tickle *v.* (使)发痒

glorious *adj.* 值得称道的；荣耀的
furrow *v.* 犁

garden. It was a woman from the family. She hummed a song he had never heard. It was the sweetest sound.

The fir tree spent several weeks listening to the woman work. She had planted seeds, and they were starting to grow. He did not know what kind of plants they were yet, but he knew he would tell them his stories. He would help the plants grow to be strong and tall, and then send them on adventures of their own.

这家的女人，她在唱着他从未听过的歌曲，这是一支最甜美的歌儿。

冷杉几周以来一直听着女人工作。她种下种子，种子已经开始生长了。他还不知道女人种的是什么种子，但他知道他会给他们讲自己的故事，他会帮助这些植物长壮、长高，然后让他们自己去历险。

13

Murdoch's Path

Chapter 1

Pat was a poor delivery boy, and all the townsfolk loved him. He was as *trustworthy* as a clock and always delivered goods and payment on time. And he always returned any *change*. He had as much work as he could handle. If it only paid well, he would have been a rich man. But Pat was so poor that when he walked on the *highway*, he kept his shoes in his pockets until he got to town. That

---

默多克的小路

第一章

　　帕特是一个贫穷的送货的男孩，城里所有的人都喜欢他。他的信誉度如同时钟一样，他送的货和付费都是准时的，而且他总是送回来任何零钱。他的工作正好是他能处理过来的。如果他的工资好一些的话，他就会成为一个富人。但是帕特太穷了，当他走在高速公路上的时候，他把鞋放进口袋里，直到进城以后再穿上。用这种方法，他的鞋不容易磨坏。

---

trustworthy *adj.* 值得信任的；可靠的　　　　　　　change *n.* 零钱
highway *n.* 公路

way, the shoes would not wear out.

One night, his deliveries had kept him so late that he rushed down the dark road, his shoes still on his feet. This is what he was saying to himself:

"A dozen balls of gray *yarn* for Mistress Murphy. Three dozen bright buttons for the tailor. Half an *ounce* of throat drops for Father Andrew." These were the *items* he had been sent to *fetch*. He repeated them so he would be sure to remember them.

Now, everyone knew that there were two ways home from town. One was the proper highway, and the other was Murdoch's Path.

一天晚上，他送货太晚了，他得在黑黑的路上快速地跑，他的鞋还穿在脚上，他对自己是这样说的：

"十二团灰色毛线给墨菲女士，三打亮色的纽扣给裁缝，半盎司喉咙滴液给安德鲁老爹。"这些就是被派出来取的东西。他重复着这些内容，这样他能确保记住。

现在，人人都知道从城里到家有两条路可走。一条是直接的高速公路，另一条是默多克小路。这条小路只是一个潮湿的、沼泽的、荆棘丛生

---

yarn *n.* 纱；纱线

item *n.* 一件商品(或物品)

ounce *n.* 盎司

fetch *v.* (去)拿来；(去)取来

The Path was nothing more than a wet, swampy, *brambly*, overgrown ditch. No one dared go there because it was *infested* with fairies. In all the years Pat had gone to and from town, he had always taken the highway. But poor Pat was so late and so deep in thought that when he came to the *fork* where the Path split off, he didn't even look up. He marched right down Murdoch's Path without even noticing.

Chapter 2

He wasn't sure how far he'd gone when suddenly a full moon came from behind the clouds. It made the land as bright as day. Pat looked up and realized he had taken the wrong turn, for right in front of him was a circle of dancing fairies. They danced around and around until Pat's feet *tingled*. Fairy music makes anyone want

---

的而又长满杂草的壕沟。没有人敢走这里，因为这里有很多的精灵。在几年的所有时间里，帕特都要进城出城，他总是走高速公路。但是可怜的帕特今天是太晚了，只想着心事儿，当他来到岔路口时，就是分成两岔的路口，他没有抬头看一下，他大步走进了默多克小路，而且还没有注意到。

第二章

他自己也搞不清走了多远，这时从云朵后面出来一轮满月。月亮使得大地像白天一样明亮。帕特抬起头一看，意识到他转错弯了，因为在他的正前方有一群小精灵在跳舞。他们一圈圈地跳着，直到帕特的脚也痒痒的。精灵的音乐会让所有的人想要跳舞的，不管天色多么晚，不管一个人

---

brambly *adj.* 灌木丛生的
fork *n.* 岔口；岔路

infest *v.* 大量滋生；大批出没于
tingle *v.* 强烈地感到

to dance, no matter how late it is and no matter how tired he is. Pat simply waited and watched. After a long time, a little man in a black hat, a green coat, and red shoes *beckoned* him into the circle.

"Won't you dance a song with us, Pat?" asked the little man, bowing till he nearly touched the ground. He didn't have far to go, for he was barely two feet high.

"I'll be proud to dance with you," replied Pat. Before he could look round, Pat jumped in the circle and began dancing as though his life depended on it.

At first, his feet felt lighter than feathers. It seemed as though he could have danced forever. But soon he grew tired and would have liked to stop, yet the fairies wouldn't let him. So he danced on and

---

有多么累。帕特只是待在那里看着。过了好长一段时间，一个戴着黑色帽子、穿着绿色外衣和红鞋子的小人，招呼他加入他们一起跳舞。

"你不想和我们跳上一曲吗，帕特？"这个小人说，他弯腰施礼已经都要贴到地上了。他不能弯得太狠，因为他本身也就两英尺高。

"与你们跳舞我会很自豪的，"帕特回答说。帕特还没有来得及左右看一下，就跳到人群中开始跳舞，就像他的生命没有舞蹈不行一样。

开始时，他觉得他的脚比羽毛还要轻，看起来好像他能永远跳下去。但是很快他就累了，想要停下来，但是精灵们不同意，所以他就跳呀跳。帕特知道自己受了咒语的控制，想着用哪个咒语解开它，但是他能想起来

---

beckon *v.* 招手示意；举手召唤

on. Pat realized that he was under a spell and tried to think of some magic words to break it. But all he could think was:

"A dozen balls of gray yarn for Mistress Murphy. Three dozen bright buttons for the tailor. Half an ounce of throat drops for Father Andrew," over and over.

It seemed to Pat that the moon had almost set below the grass by the time the fairies finished dancing. But he couldn't be sure with all the *spinning* and running around. One thing he was sure of, though. He had danced every bit of leather off the *soles* of his shoes. His feet were *blistered* so that he could hardly stand. All the little fairies stood and held their sides while they laughed at him.

的只是这个：

"十二团灰色毛线给墨菲女士，三打亮色的纽扣给裁缝，半盎司喉咙滴液给安德鲁老爹。"一遍遍地重复着。

帕特觉得月亮快要落到草以下了，这时精灵们才会停止跳舞。但是他还不敢确定，因为所有的精灵都在旋转和转圈。但是，有一个东西他可以确定，他把鞋上的皮子跳掉了，他的脚上起满了泡，所以他几乎都不敢站着了。所有的小精灵们都站在那里，叉着腰笑他。

spin *v.* (使)快速旋转
blister *v.* (使)起水泡；起泡

sole *n.* 鞋底

Chapter 3

At last, the fairy with the green coat and the red shoes stepped up to him. "Don't worry about it, Pat," he said. "I'll lend you my red shoes until morning, for you seem to be a good-natured sort of boy."

Well, Pat looked at the fairy man's shoes. They were the size of a baby's. He didn't wish to be rude, so he said, "Thank you, sir. If you would be kind enough to put them on my feet for me, perhaps you won't *spoil* their fine shape."

Pat thought that if the fairy man put them on Pat's big feet, it wouldn't be Pat's fault if the tiny shoes broke. So he sat down on the side of the Path, and the fairy man put the shoes on Pat's feet. As

第三章

最后，穿绿色外衣、红色鞋子的精灵走到他的面前，"不要着急，帕特，"他说，"我把我的红鞋子借给你，早晨还我，因为你看起来是本质非常好的男孩子。"

好吧，帕特看了一眼这个精灵的鞋子，大小适合婴儿。他不希望表现得太粗鲁，于是他说，"谢谢你，先生，如果你能帮我穿在脚上的话，那就非常感谢了，也许你不会弄坏鞋子漂亮的外形。"

帕特想，如果精灵把鞋穿在他的脚上，鞋撑破了，也不是他的错误。于是他坐在小路的边儿上，精灵给他穿鞋。他们刚一接触到帕特的脚，鞋

spoil *v.* 破坏；毁掉

soon as they touched Pat's feet, the shoes grew to just the perfect size and fit him better than his socks. In addition, when he stood up, he didn't feel his blisters at all.

"Make sure you bring them back to the Path at sunrise," said the little man. Then Pat climbed the ditch and looked around. All around the roots of the bushes and in the grass were jewels and *pearls*.

"Do you want to help yourself, Pat, or will you take what I give you?" asked the little man.

"I'll take whatever you give me and be thankful," said Pat, remembering his manners. The fairy man picked a large handful of yellow flowers from the bushes and filled Pat's pockets.

就长大了，刚好适合他脚的大小，比他的袜子还合适。另外，当他站起来时，他没有感到脚上水泡的疼痛。

"一定要在太阳升起前把鞋还给我，"这个小人说。帕特爬出了水沟，向周围看了一下。在树根的周围和草丛中，到处是珠宝和珍珠。

"你想自己弄吗，帕特？或者你能拿我给你的东西吗？"这个小人问。

"我只拿你给我的东西，而且非常感谢，"帕特说，他还记着自己的风度。这个精灵从树丛中摘了一大把黄色的花，放在了帕特的衣袋里。

pearl *n.* 珍珠

"Make sure you keep those, Pat," he said. Pat would have liked some of the jewels, but he said nothing. "Oh, and before you go, let me *polish* those shoes for you."

So Pat lifted each foot. The little man *dusted* the shoes off by breathing on them and *rubbing* them with the tail of his little green coat. "Home!" said the little man with a magical snap of his fingers. In an instant, Pat found himself standing on his own doorstep with all his deliveries safe around him.

Chapter 4

The next morning, Pat got up before sunrise and carried the shoes back to the Path. As Pat came up, the little man looked over the edge of the ditch.

"记住一定要留好这些东西，帕特，"他说，帕特本来想拿一些珠宝，但他什么都没说，"噢，在你走之前，我给你的鞋擦亮吧。"

于是帕特抬起脚，这个小人用嘴吹掉鞋上的灰尘，用绿色衣服的后摆擦鞋。"家！"这个小人一边用手指打一个响一边说。马上帕特发现自己站在自己家门前的台阶上了，他送的货都安全的在他的周围。

第四章

第二天早晨，帕特在太阳没有出来前起床，带着这双鞋回到小路。帕特到来的时候，那个小人在水沟的边上向外张望着。

---

polish *v.* 擦亮；摩光
rub *v.* 擦；磨

dust *v.* 擦去……的灰尘；擦灰

"Top o' the morning to you," said Pat. "Here are your shoes."

"Why, thank you, Pat. Have you had a chance to take a look at those flowers yet?"

"No, sir," replied Pat. "I came straight here when I woke up this morning."

"Make sure you look when you get back, Pat. And good luck to you." And with that, the little man disappeared. When Pat got home, he took a look at the little yellow *blossoms*. He had to rub his eyes twice. They had all turned to *pure* gold pieces.

Well, the first thing Pat did was to go to the shoemaker to have him make a beautiful pair of new shoes. And being a kind boy, he told the curious shoemaker the whole story. The shoemaker began to feel greedy. He wondered if he could go to the Path and dance with the fairies that night.

"祝你早晨最最好，"帕特说，"这是你的鞋子。"

"噢，谢谢你，帕特，你有没有机会看一下那些花儿呢?"

"没有呢，先生，"帕特回答说，"我早晨醒来是直接到这里来的。"

"回去之后一定要看呀，帕特。祝你好运。"说完这句话，那个小人就消失了。帕特回到了家，看了一眼那些小黄花，他得把眼睛擦两遍，那些花都变成了一块块金子。

好吧，帕特做的第一件事情是找鞋匠给他做一双漂亮的新鞋。因为他是一个善良的孩子，所以把整个故事告诉了好奇的鞋匠。鞋匠开始变得贪

---

blossom *n.* 花朵；花簇

pure *adj.* 完全的；纯粹的

Chapter 5

The shoemaker found his way to the Path all right. And when he got there, the fairies were dancing. But instead of waiting politely, he *barged* right in and began to dance with them. He danced the soles of his shoes off, as Pat did, and the fairy man lent him the red shoes. When the shoemaker came out of the ditch, he saw the jewels and pearls *scattered* in the grass. "Will you help yourself, or will you take what I give ye?" asked the little man.

"Why, I think I'll help myself, if you please," said the shoemaker. And he *stuffed* every pocket, plus his socks, with precious stones. The little man made him promise to return the shoes in the morning and sent him home in a *twinkling*.

When the shoemaker got home, he immediately pulled the jewels

梦起来，他在想是不是他也可以晚上到那个小路上，与精灵们跳舞。

第五章

鞋匠顺利地找到了去小路的路，他到了那里，精灵们正在跳舞。他没有礼貌地在旁边等着，而是马上靠了上来，与他们一起跳舞。他把他的鞋底跳掉了，这与帕特相同，精灵把自己的红鞋借给了他。当鞋匠走出水沟时，他看到草丛间有很多的珠宝和珍珠。"你是自己拿，还是我拿给你？"小人问道。

"为什么呢，我想我可以自己拿，如果你同意的话，"鞋匠说。然后他把所有的衣兜，还有袜子塞满了宝石。小人要求他答应早晨一定还鞋，

barge *v.* 冲撞；闯入　　　　　　　　scatter *v.* 使散开
stuff *v.* 装满；塞满　　　　　　　　twinkling *n.* 瞬间；一眨眼

from his pockets. But not a single jewel remained; there was nothing but a *heap* of ordinary pebbles. The shoemaker swore and *stomped*, and then he thought to himself that he would keep the little man's shoes. "Who knows what magic is in them?" he thought.

So he made a tiny pair of red shoes just like the fairy shoes. He covered the real shoes with black polish, so they couldn't be recognized. Then at sunrise he went back to the Path. Just as before, the fairy man appeared at the edge of the ditch.

Chapter 6

"Top of the morning to you," said the shoemaker. "Here are your shoes." He handed the fairy man the pair he had made. The little

---

一眨眼就把他送回家了。

鞋匠到家以后，他马上就从衣兜里取出珠宝，但没有一个珠宝，什么都没有，只是平常的石子。鞋匠大骂，跺脚，然后他想，他把小鞋留下，"谁知道这里面有什么魔法呢？"他这样想着。

于是，他做了一双小红鞋，与精灵的鞋完全一样。他用黑色上光漆涂在了真鞋上面，这样就看不出来了。在太阳升起之前，他回到了小路，与以前是一样的，精灵人出现在水沟的边儿上。

第六章

"祝你早晨最最好！"鞋匠说，"这是你的鞋，"说着他把自己做的

---

heap *n.* 一堆；大量

stamp *v.* 跺脚

man looked at them, but he said nothing, and he did not put them on.

"Have you looked at the things I gave you last night?" said the little man.

"Oh, no. I came here as soon as I woke up," lied the shoemaker.

"Be sure to look when you get back," said the little man. And then the shoemaker *grinned*. He was sure that the fairy man had just *uttered* the magic words that would turn the pebbles back into jewels.

"Ah, sir," said the fairy man, "I believe there's a bit of dust on your shoes. Let me polish them for you."

那双鞋递给了精灵。小人看了一眼那双鞋，什么都没说，也没穿在脚上。

"你看过我昨晚给你的东西了吗？"小人问道。

"噢，没有，我一醒来就来这里了，"鞋匠撒谎说。

"回到家里一定要看一下，"小人说。这时鞋匠笑了一下，他确定这个精灵刚刚说出的咒语，是会把石子变成珠宝的。

"啊，先生，"精灵说，"我看你的鞋上有一些灰尘，我替你擦一下吧。"

"他的意思是我马上就能回家了，"鞋匠想，但是小人吹了一下他

---

grin v. 露齿而笑；咧着嘴笑

utter v. 出声；说；讲

"That means I'll be home in an instant," thought the shoemaker. But the little man breathed on his shoes and *muttered* some words the shoemaker couldn't hear. Soon, the shoemaker's feet began to tingle. Then they *itched*, and then they burned. Finally, he began to dance, and he danced all around the Path. The fairy man laughed and laughed, holding his sides. The shoemaker danced until he cried out from *exhaustion*, but the fairies *drove* him *away*. Where he went, nobody knows, but some say they've seen the greedy shoemaker dancing from sunset to sunrise around Murdoch's Path.

的鞋，小声说了一些鞋匠听不见的话。这时鞋匠觉得脚痒痒的，然后就更痒，再后来就是发烫。最后他开始跳舞，他绕着小路跳着。精灵笑呀笑，叉着腰笑。鞋匠不停地跳着，直到他累得大叫了起来，但是精灵把他赶走了。赶到哪里了，没有人知道，但有人说看到这个贪婪的鞋匠在默多克小路上从太阳升起跳舞一直跳到太阳落山。

---

mutter *v.* 嘀咕；嘟囔
exhaustion *n.* 筋疲力尽；疲惫不堪

itch *v.* 发痒
drive away 使离去；赶跑

The Wall

Once upon a time, further back than anyone can remember, two kingdoms got into an argument. No one could *recall* what it was about, for it was ages upon ages ago, but everyone was so *furious* about it that they decided to build a wall between their lands. It was taller than anyone could climb and longer than anyone could travel.

The wall kept the two kingdoms *utterly* separate, though no

墙

很久很久以前，两个王国争执不休。没人想得起来争吵的原因，因为时间实在是太久了，但是大家都很气愤，所以人们决定在两国领土间修一座墙。这座墙高到任何人都无法攀爬，长到任何人都无法行进到头。

尽管没人能够想起两个王国不能继续成为邻国的原因，这座墙却把它

---

recall *v.* 回忆起；回想起　　　　　　　furious *adj.* 狂怒的；暴怒的
utterly *adv.* 完全地；彻底地

one could remember just why they couldn't stand to be neighbors anymore. Nonetheless, when *cracks* appeared in the wall, people repaired them, and when streams wore away holes under the wall, the people quickly filled them in with earth and stones. "We don't want those *scoundrels* from the other side coming over here," they said.

So much time had passed since anyone had seen the other kingdom, no one was sure what it looked like anymore. But they assumed there must be some reason for the wall being there. There must be something about the people of that other kingdom, either good or bad, if the wall was needed to keep them out. "Or is the wall there to keep us out of their kingdom?" the people wondered. Eventually, people began to tell stories about what had become of the other kingdom.

们完全分开了。尽管如此，当墙出现裂缝的时候，人们把墙修补好；当小河把墙冲出洞的时候，人们迅速用泥土和石头把洞填上。他们说："我们可不想让那边的坏蛋过来。"

自从两个王国的人们互不相见很久以后，谁也不知道对方是什么样子。但他们认为修这座墙一定有原因。墙把两个王国分开，无论如何一定是另一个王国的原因。人们怀疑：或者是这座墙把我们和他们的王国隔开了？最后，人们开始讲述另一个王国现在是什么样子的故事。

---

crack *n.* 破裂；断裂   scoundrel *n.* 无赖；恶棍

One story said that the other kingdom had *bred* an army of *hideous*, fire-breathing monsters. They treated the monsters very cruelly, and kept them angry all the time.

"The monsters will cross the wall and *invade* us any day now," the people shouted. "The other kingdom is evil and cruel."

Another story said that aliens had come from the sky one day and *blasted* the other kingdom to powder. Then the aliens took everything that remained, loaded it on their ships, and flew away, leaving an open land. "The aliens are on our side," said the people. "They have destroyed the other kingdom and left the land for us. The aliens are all-knowing, and they obviously proved us right about that other kingdom."

有一个故事说另一个王国组建了一支丑陋的喷火怪兽军队。他们残忍地对待这些怪兽，让他们一直保持狂暴的状态。

人们大声地说："怪兽们随时都会穿过墙入侵我们。他们王国邪恶又残忍。"

另一个故事说有一天来自天空的外星人把另一个王国炸得粉碎。然后外星人把残留的所有东西都装上飞船，离开这里，只留下一片空旷的土地。人们说："现在外星人是我们这边的。他们已经摧毁了另一个王国，把土地留给了我们。外星人无所不知，显然他们证明了我们对另一个王国的所作所为是正确的。"

---

breed v. 培育；教育　　　　　　　hideous adj. 十分丑陋的；令人厌恶的
invade v. 入侵；侵袭　　　　　　　blast v. 把……炸成碎片；爆破；炸毁

But there was another story, one that was much more disturbing. Most people claimed that they did not believe it, but in their hearts, they wondered whether it might be true. Over the unnumbered years, the other kingdom had become a *paradise*. The streets were paved with candy, the trees were made of chocolate, and everyone was *blissfully* happy. "And we sit here working all day, with nothing but regular bread, meat, and vegetables to eat," *grumbled* the people. "That greedy kingdom just wants to keep the paradise to themselves."

No matter which story people told, it only made them *despise* the other kingdom more and more. "Evil attackers will come any day now!" cried some. "The supreme alien race proved that they were terrible and deserved to die," shouted others. "They look down upon

---

　　然而还有另一个令人不安的故事。大多数人宣称他们不相信，但是在他们的内心里，还是怀疑其真实性。这么多年过去了，另一个王国成了一片乐园：街道由糖果铺成，树木是巧克力做成的，每个人都快乐幸福。人们抱怨说："我们坐在这里整天工作，食物单调到只有面包、肉和蔬菜。那个贪婪的王国只想自己在乐园里享受。"

　　无论人们讲的哪个故事，都让他们越来越鄙视另一个王国。有人喊叫着："邪恶的攻击者随时都会来！"其他人大声地说："至高无上的外星人种族证实了他们的可怕，他们应该死。"还有人喃喃自语："他们看不起我们，把我们当成可怜的流氓。"但是没人知道确切的情况。

---

paradise　*n.* 乐土；乐园　　　　　　blissfully　*adv.* 极乐地；幸福地
grumble　*v.* 咕哝；发牢骚　　　　　despise　*v.* 鄙视；看不起

us as poor *ruffans*," muttered others. But no one knew for sure.

But the children of the kingdom were tired of hating. "How can we hate something if we don't know what it is?" asked Richard. "I say we discover who's on the other side of the wall. Once we learn about them, maybe we can figure out what the argument was, and we might even be able to end the fight. Then we can finally get rid of this ugly old wall."

"But how would we find out?" asked Mary. "No one can see over the wall or travel around it."

"I've got it!" shouted Frederic. "We'll buy a parrot, the smartest one in the land," explained Frederic. "We'll teach it to speak and send it over the wall with a message for the people on the other

---

　　但是孩子们厌倦了憎恨。理查德问："我们为什么要憎恨我们不知道的事情呢？我说我们来讨论一下墙那边的人。如果我们了解他们，也许就可以理解争吵，甚至结束战争了。最终我们就可以拆除这座丑陋的旧墙。"

　　玛丽问："但是我们怎么才能知道呢？没有人能看到墙那边或是到墙的那边去。"

　　弗雷德里克大声说："我有办法了！"他解释道："我们买一只鹦鹉，它是陆地上最聪明的。我们教它说话，让它带着给墙那边人的消息从

---

ruffan *n.* 暴徒；恶棍

side."

"Let's ask them why they have monsters coming to kill us," suggested Mary.

"We can only ask them something if there's someone to ask," objected Richard. "But what if the aliens *demolished* them?"

"Yeah," said Mary, "and if it's a perfect paradise, they'll only shoot the parrot for being from the poor, ugly side of the wall."

"Hold on a minute," said Frederic. "The whole point of this is that we don't know what's over there. We're sending the parrot to find out. Perhaps we should send a simple message, something like 'Who are you?' Then we can't really get into trouble."

墙上飞过去。"

　　玛丽建议说："我们问问他们为什么让怪兽来杀我们。"

　　理查德反对说："我们就问问他们有没有人要问我们问题。但是如果外星人摧毁了他们怎么办呢？"

　　玛丽说："是啊，如果那里是美妙的乐园，他们会开枪射击来自贫困丑陋的墙这一边的鹦鹉。"

　　弗雷德里克说："等等，最重要的是我们不知道墙那边的情况。我们打算放鹦鹉飞过去了解情况。也许我们应该发送简单的消息，比如你是

demolish *v.* 拆毁；拆除；打败

So the three children *purchased* the most intelligent parrot they could find. In no time, it spoke fluently, and they sent it to see what had become of the kingdom behind the wall.

"Don't let the other kingdom know that you come from our side," Richard said.

"Yeah, I don't want those people knowing who we are," Mary said.

"They'll only come over and kill us," said Richard.

Frederic just sighed.

But the bird was even wiser than the children supposed. It understood that the people feared and hated what was on the other side of the wall, even though they weren't sure what it was. Off it

---

谁，这样我们就不会有麻烦。

于是三个孩子买了一只他们能够找到的最聪明的鹦鹉。很快鹦鹉就可以流利地说话了，他们放飞鹦鹉去查看墙后面的王国现在的样子。

理查德说："别让他们王国知道你来自我们这边。"

玛丽说："对，我不想让那些人知道我们是谁。"

理查德说："他们会来杀我们的。"

弗雷德里克只是在叹气。

这只鹦鹉比孩子们想象的聪明得多。它知道人们害怕和憎恨墙的那

---

purchase *v.* 购买；采购

flew over the wall, and after three very long days, it returned."Tell us what you saw," Frederic asked, anxiously.

"I saw people," said the parrot, "and they all looked very sad. I flew down into a tree and listened to them. They said they regretted ever having the argument, and they wished they had never built this wall. They only hoped that they could be friends with your kingdom again."

The children were *astonished*, and a little ashamed. They had never *suspected* that the people on the other side of the wall might want to be friends.

"Send a message to the other kingdom," Mary said quickly. "Tell

---

边，尽管他们也不清楚墙那边的情况。从它飞过墙，过了漫长的三天才飞回来。弗雷德里克不安地问："告诉我们你看到了什么。"

鹦鹉说："我看到的人们都很难过。我飞到一棵树上，听到他们说他们很后悔发生争吵，他们希望从来没修过这座墙。他们只希望再次和你们王国的人成为朋友。"

孩子们很吃惊，感到了一点点惭愧。他们从来没有觉得墙那边的人想和他们成为朋友。

玛丽立刻说道："给他们王国发消息，告诉他们我们想和他们成为朋友。无论如何，我们对争吵感到抱歉。"

---

astonish *adj.* 感到十分惊讶；吃惊   suspect *v.* 猜想；怀疑

them that we want to be friends, and that we're also really sorry about the argument, whatever it was."

The parrot seemed to *wink* to itself. You see, it had already told the other kingdom that the children were sending a message asking for peace. The people there were just like the people in this kingdom—they did not know what lay behind the wall, but they hated it anyway. The other kingdom had been as shocked and ashamed of their *hatred* as the children had been. In no time, the wall was gone, and the two kingdoms were friends again. They forgot all about their argument, whatever it was.

　　鹦鹉似乎眨了眨眼睛。它已经告诉另一个王国孩子们要发出请求和平的消息。那里的人们和这个王国的人们一样——他们不知道墙那边的情况，只是憎恨。知道了孩子们的行为后，另一个王国的人也像孩子们一样为自己的敌意感到震惊和羞愧。墙很快拆除了，两个王国的人们又成为朋友。不管怎么样，他们忘记了过去的争吵。

---

wink *v.* 眨眼   hatred *n.* 仇恨；憎恨；厌恶

15

The Squire's Bride

Feeling Lonely

Long ago and far away, a rich *squire* rode out to look over his land. He watched his field workers *harvesting hay*.

The squire smiled, for he would soon be able to sell the hay for gold.

A red leaf landed on the squire's nose. Then, more and more leaves floated in the air. He *frowned*, remembering how long and

---

乡绅的新娘

感觉到了孤独

在很久以前，一个遥远的地方有一个乡绅，骑着马视察自己的田地，他看着这些田地里的工人们收干草。

乡绅笑了，因为他很快就会把这些草卖掉，换来金子。

有一片红色的叶子落在了乡绅的鼻子上，又有很多的叶子飘到空中。他皱一下眉头，想起来冬天是多么的漫长而又孤独。

---

squire *n.* 乡绅；大地主
hay *n.* 干草；草料

harvest *v.* 收割；收获
frown *v.* 皱眉；蹙额

lonely winter was.

The squire spotted a lovely girl in the field. "I shall make her my wife," he thought.

"Will you marry me?" he asked. "You will have a big house and wear beautiful clothes," he said, but the girl refused his offer.

A Promise Made

The squire was angry. He promised to pay her father's *debt* if the father could get his daughter to marry the squire.

"*Arrange* the wedding," said her father, "and when you are ready, *send for* my daughter."

乡绅看到田野中有一个可爱的女孩，"我一定要娶这个女孩当妻子，"他想。

"你能嫁给我吗?"他问。"你会有很大的房子，还能穿漂亮的衣服，"他说，但女孩子拒绝了他的请求。

做出承诺

乡绅生气了，他承诺说，如果女孩父亲同意把女儿嫁给他，他就会替他们偿还所有的债务。

"那就安排婚礼吧，"女孩的父亲说，"然后，你可以随时来接我的女儿。"

---

debt *n.* 债务；欠款　　　　　　　　　　　arrange *v.* 安排
send for 请某人来

The squire's cooks spent days making a feast, and the maids cleaned his big house to a shine.

He invited all the neighbors and hired the *parson*.

When everything was ready, he sent a boy to the girl's father.

"Tell him to send what he promised," the squire ordered, "and be quick."

A Promise Fulfilled

The boy hurried to the farmer's house. "My master said to send what you promised, and hurry."

"Yes, yes," said the man, "she's in the field. Take her with you."

The boy found the girl *raking* hay. He said, "I'm here to fetch what

---

乡绅的厨师们整天都在准备宴会，女仆们把房子擦得锃光瓦亮。

乡绅向所有的邻居都发出了邀请，还雇了一个教区牧师。

事情都准备好以后，乡绅派一个男孩子去女孩子的父亲家。

"告诉他把答应的东西送过来吧，"乡绅指示说，"而且要快。"

兑现承诺

男孩子急匆匆地来到农夫房子前，"我的主人说，送去你答应的东西吧，而且要快。"

"是，好的。"农夫说，"她就在田地里，把她带走吧。"

小男孩在田地里找到了这个姑娘，她正在耙干草。他说，"我来带走

---

parson *n.* 教区牧师

rake *v.* 耙；梳理

your father promised my master."

"Oh, yes," she said, with a smile, "He means the little *bay mare*. She's at the edge of the field."

The boy jumped on the mare's back and rode fast to the squire's home. "She's outside by the door," he told the squire.

"Take her upstairs to her room," the squire said.

The *lad* shook his head, but he knew better than to argue with the squire. He got seven men to push and pull the mare up the stairs.

你父亲答应我的主人的东西。"

"啊，是的，"她笑了一下说，"他说的是那匹栗色的小母马，正在地头吃草呢。"

小男孩子跳上这匹母马，飞快地奔向乡绅的家里，"就在门外面，"他告诉乡绅。

"带她到房间去吧。"乡绅说。

小男孩摇了摇头，但是他知道没有必要与乡绅争论这些。他找了七个人连推带拉地把母马弄到了楼上。

---

bay *adj.* 深棕色的；枣红色的
lad *n.* 男孩儿；少年

mare *n.* 母马

The Big Event

When the women came to dress the bride, they stretched and *tugged* on the gown. They put flowers around her neck and a crown on her head. They pulled *satin* slippers on her front hooves.

The music began to play. Guests turned to watch the door where the squire waited for his bride. There was a great *clatter* on the stairs, for the bride had only two satin slippers.

The door opened.

The squire never went *courting* again.

盛典

女人们来给新娘穿衣服，她们把衣服拉一拉，塞一塞，把花装饰在母马的脖子上和头上，她们把缎子鞋穿在马的蹄子上。

音乐开始演奏，客人们转身注视着大门，在这里乡绅等待着新娘。楼梯里传来沉重地嗒嗒的脚步声，因为新娘只有两只缎子鞋。

门开了。

此后乡绅再也没有求过婚。

---

tug v. 拉；拽　　　　　　　　　　　satin *adj.* 缎子似的
clatter n. 噔噔声　　　　　　　　　court v. 求婚

16

The Castaway Pines

The *Cast*:

NARRATOR

POPPA PINE

MOMMA PINE

BABY PINE

LOGGER

NARRATOR:

松林余生

人物：

旁白

松树爸爸

松树妈妈

松树宝宝

伐木工人

旁白：

cast *n.* 人物；演员

Deep in the woods stands a family of three *pine* trees. Their branches are deep green and their *limbs* are straight. Two of the pines are fully grown, but the third is tiny—barely more than a *shrub*. Most of the forest has been cut down around them. The larger evergreen trees have been harvested, and they are the last.

The sleeping pines have their heads bowed and their eyes closed. The gentle sound of whispering wind blows through their branches.

The Logger discovers the three pine trees, standing out in the nearly empty forest.

LOGGER:

Wow! Three pines, castaways, in a sea of evergreens. I never would have known they were here, until we harvested the Douglas firs and the blue *spruce*. Well, have I got a use for them!

在森林深处住着松树一家三口，它们的枝干挺拔，枝叶呈深绿色。其中两棵松树已经完全长成，另一棵是还没有长大的小树。它们周围的大部分树木和那些高大的常青树都已经被砍伐，就剩下这几棵松树了。

熟睡的松树低着头，闭着眼睛，微风从松树的枝头轻轻拂过，听似浅吟低唱。

这三棵松树在这个近乎荒芜的森林里十分显眼，一位伐木工人发现了它们。

伐木工人：

哇！这里竟然有三棵松树，真是"松林余生"啊！要不是我们刚刚在

---

pine *n.* 松树
shrub *n.* 灌木

limb *n.* (树的)大枝；主枝
spruce *n.* 云杉

123

NARRATOR:

The Logger rushes away, as the tallest of the three pines shakes himself awake.

POPPA PINE:

Oh, what a wonderful, *brisk* winter's morning. No snow yet, but it's still early winter. I love snow. *Tickles* my boughs.

NARRATOR:

Poppa Pine stretches, as well as a tree can stretch, and looks around.

这砍伐了道格拉斯冷杉和蓝叶云杉，我怎么也不会在这儿遇到它们，嗯，得把它们派上用场！

旁白：

伐木工人急匆匆地离开了，这时，长得最高大的那棵松树摇晃着身体醒来了。

松树爸爸：

哦，多么美好的早上啊，虽然没有下雪，但毕竟进入冬天了。我太喜欢雪了，落在树枝上，就像是在给我抓痒痒。

旁白：

---

brisk *adj.* 轻快的；生气勃勃的   tickle *v.* (使)发痒

POPPA PINE:

Oh my, oh my! *Psst*! Momma? Are you awake?

NARRATOR:

Momma Pine shakes her boughs and *yawns*. She looks down at the sleeping baby pine.

MOMMA PINE:

Yes, Poppa, now I am awake. Oh, isn't it the cutest thing? Seems like only yesterday that it was just a *cone* hanging in my branches.

NARRATOR:

松树爸爸尽情地伸着懒腰，向四周望去。

松树爸爸：

天啊，天啊！喂，树妈妈，你醒了吗？

旁白：

松树妈妈晃动着身体，打了个哈欠，又低头看了看正在睡觉的树宝宝。

松树妈妈：

树爸爸，我睡醒了。哦，看我们的宝宝多可爱啊，当初还是生长在我树枝上的一颗松果，这一切就好像发生在昨天一样。

---

psst *int.* (用于引起注意的声音)嘘；嘶   yawn *v.* 打哈欠

cone *n.* (松树或冷杉的)球果

Poppa Pine looks nervously over his shoulder.

POPPA PINE:

We may have a problem. I mean, a really big problem.

NARRATOR:

Momma Pine looks at the baby, distracted. Eyes opened wide, she looks around but sees nothing.

MOMMA PINE:

And just what could that be, Poppa? It's not those *pesky* root *weevils*, is it? I just hate when they come buzzing around. They are so boring. I want to think that all creatures have their place in Nature's

---

旁白：
树爸爸紧张地转头看着身后。

树爸爸：
我们可能有麻烦了，大麻烦。

旁白：
树妈妈正全神贯注地看着宝宝，听到树爸爸的话抬起了头，睁大双眼向周围看了看，但是什么都没有发现。

树妈妈：
树爸爸，你发现了什么吗？不会是那些可恶的象鼻虫吧？我讨厌它们

---

pesky *adj.* 恼人的；讨厌的   weevil *n.* 象鼻虫

plan, but I don't know — weevils just get under my *bark*. Then it's nothing but itch, itch, itch.

POPPA PINE:

No, Momma, it's not the root weevils. It's much worse than that. It's the loggers.

MOMMA PINE:

The loggers? Are you sure? It just can't be the loggers. We are hidden so deep in this sea of evergreens. Are you sure it's the loggers?

在我身边飞来飞去的，太讨厌了。我是应该这么想：万事万物在大自然中自有其生存的方式，但是真是没法这么想——象鼻虫钻进我的皮肤里，让我感觉实在痒得受不了。

松树爸爸：

不是的，树妈妈，我说的不是象鼻虫，要是象鼻虫还好点，是伐木工人要来了。

松树妈妈：

伐木工人？你确定吗？不会是伐木工人的。不会吧，我们可是隐蔽在森林深处，你确定他们会发现我们吗？

---

bark *n.* 树皮

POPPA PINE:

Shhhh! You're going to wake the baby. Yes, I'm sure. Look, there aren't any big evergreens left around us. They're all gone! Next thing you know the loggers will come to *chop* us down, too.

MOMMA PINE:

But good loggers or bad loggers?

POPPA PINE:

I don't know. One way or the other, we will be used for something. Could be something good — maybe a wooden chair or a wooden *porch* or ... a Christmas tree.

松树爸爸:

嘘！你这么大声会把宝宝吵醒的。我真的看见有人了。你看，我们周围的常青树都不见了，接下来就轮到我们了，伐木工也会把我们砍断的。

松树妈妈:

来的像是好人还是坏人啊？

松树爸爸:

不知道，来的不管是好人坏人，我们还不是被人们拿去做东西。命好的话，就去当个木椅或门廊……或者我们会成为圣诞树。

---

chop *v.* 砍；   porch *n.* 门廊；门厅

MOMMA PINE:

Oh, Poppa, don't get that hope up and running. Only the best of the best can become Christmas trees. I have always been *realistic*—maybe a hand-carved rocking chair or an end table. It won't be so bad. Actually, it may not be bad at all.

POPPA PINE:

But it could be very bad.

MOMMA PINE:

Poppa, I do declare. You do *exaggerate* so! It just makes my *sap* run cold when you talk like that. What possibly could be worse than

---

松树妈妈：

天啊，树爸爸，可别痴心妄想了，只有最好的松树才会被用来做圣诞树呢。我的想法一直很现实，也许只会用我们做一把手工雕刻的摇椅或者一张茶几罢了。不会这么惨的，或者根本就什么事都没有。

松树爸爸：

但是也可能会出大事。

松树妈妈：

树爸爸，我现在很认真地说，你太夸张了！你这个腔调，真让人毛骨悚然，不就是把我们砍伐下来做原木使用吗，还能更糟吗？

---

realistic　*adj.*　现实的；实际的　　　　exaggerate　*v.*　夸张；夸大；言过其实
sap　*n.*　液；汁

a timber logger?

POPPA PINE:

It could be . . . *presto* loggers.

MOMMA PINE:

Presto loggers who will . . .

POPPA PINE:

. . . *grind* us into *sawdust* and make presto logs out of us!

NARRATOR:

The shouting wakes up Baby Pine.

BABY PINE:

What's going on? How come you're yelling?

松树爸爸：
更糟的是……伐木做燃料的人。
松树妈妈：
那些人会……
松树爸爸：
……把我们碾磨成木屑，然后再把我们做成燃料！
旁白：
爸爸讲话的声音太大了，惊醒了树宝宝。
松树宝宝：
怎么了？你们为什么这么大喊大叫的？

---

presto *adj.* 迅速的   grind *v.* 磨碎；碾碎
sawdust *n.* 锯末；锯木屑

MOMMA PINE:

We're not yelling, dear. Now *suck* some *nutrients* from your roots, collect a little sunshine with your leaves, and make some food while you go back to sleep.

BABY PINE:

Oh, Mom! I don't want to go back to sleep. Today you *promised* me you'd teach me how to make the wind sing through my branches.

POPPA PINE:

Look, Baby, we've got some grown-up tree things to discuss. It would just be better if you were asleep, that's all.

松树妈妈：

没有啊，亲爱的，让你的根须吸取点养分，用叶子收集些阳光，一边睡觉一边合成些养料吧。

松树宝宝：

妈妈，我不想睡觉，今天你答应过我会教我如何让微风伴着枝杈唱歌。

松树爸爸：

听着，孩子，我们大人有重要的事情商量，你最好还是去睡觉，知道吗？

松树宝宝：

我才不听呢。我不听，我不听，我不听，我什么都没听见。

---

suck *v.* 吸
promise *v.* 充诺；许诺

nutrient *n.* 营养素；营养物

132

BABY PINE:

I just won't listen. Ninner, ninner, ninner. I can't hear you.

MOMMA PINE:

Stop it!

NARRATOR:

Baby Pine's lower lip begins to tremble. It presses its branches to its eyes.

POPPA PINE:

Oh, don't cry. I just can't *handle* crying! Windstorms. Snowstorms. Anything but crying.

松树妈妈:
别闹了!
旁白:
松树宝宝的下嘴唇开始微微颤动,同时用树枝蒙上了双眼。
松树爸爸:
天啊,不要哭了。我真是害怕别人在我面前哭,暴风暴雪都难不倒我,就怕这个。
松树妈妈:
我的小宝宝,别哭了,好了,是妈妈不对。

handle *v.* 处理;对付

MOMMA PINE:

It's okay, little seedling. It's okay. Momma's sorry!

NARRATOR: *Sobbing*, Baby Pine slowly sinks, branches leaning to the ground as it falls asleep, exhausted from crying.

POPPA PINE:

Is it asleep?

MOMMA PINE:

Yes, finally. I don't know if I want any more *saplings*. Having pine cones is one thing, but maintaining a nursery of seedlings is *exhausting*.

旁白：

树宝宝哭着哭着，声音渐渐低了下去。它哭得累了，树枝向地面垂下来，睡着了。

松树爸爸：

它睡着了吗？

松树妈妈：

是啊，终于睡了。我不知道以后会不会生树宝宝了，它们是松果的时候是挺好的，将它们抚养长大真是累人啊！

---

sob *v.* 抽噎；啜泣
exhausting *adj.* 使筋疲力尽的，使耗尽的

sapling *n.* 幼树

POPPA PINE:

Shhh! Something's coming.

NARRATOR:

Both older pines freeze in place, silently. The Logger returns, carrying his ax.

NARRATOR:

The Logger walks up to the trees and leans the ax against his leg. He spits on his *palms* and rubs them together. He *grips* the ax and looks at the trees. He decides that the biggest tree is the one he wants and tries to swing his ax, but the little tree is in the way.

松树爸爸：

嘘！有人过来了。

旁白：

树爸爸和树妈妈立刻安静下来，一动不动。原来是伐木工拿着斧子回来了。

旁白：

伐木工走到松树跟前，把斧子靠在腿上。他"呸"地向掌心吐了一口唾沫，然后搓了搓双手，拿起斧子看着这几棵树。他认为那棵最大的松树正是他想要的，于是准备挥斧，但是那棵小树正好挡在前面。他试图绕到

palm *n.* 手掌；手心   grip *v.* 紧握；紧抓

He tries to work around it, but no matter how he stands, he cannot swing the ax. He becomes increasingly *frustrated*.

LOGGER:

Stupid shrub!

NARRATOR:

He grabs Baby Pine. Holding it up by its top, he lifts his ax to chop the little tree down.

POPPA PINE:

Hey, there! I wouldn't do that, if I were you.

小树的旁边，但是不管站在哪里，他都找不到挥斧的角度，于是越来越垂头丧气。

　　伐木工人：
　　讨厌的小树！
　　旁白：
　　伐木工一把抓住小树的树梢，扬起斧头，准备将小树砍掉。
　　松树爸爸：
　　嘿！如果我是你，我可不会这么做。

---

frustrated　*adj.*　沮丧；懊丧

LOGGER:

Who said that?

NARRATOR:

There is nothing but the sound of wind. Again he starts to swing the ax.

MOMMA PINE:

You do that and I'll fall on you so hard they will never find you.

LOGGER:

伐木工人：

是谁在说话？

旁白：

并没有人讲话，只能听到风声。于是伐木工再次挥起斧头。

松树妈妈：

如果你敢将斧子砍下去，我就狠狠地压在你身上，让你从此在这个世上消失。

伐木工人：

What is going on? Who said that?

NARRATOR:

The two *adult* trees bring their branches together, forming an *impenetrable* barrier that *shields* Baby Pine from the Logger's ax.

MOMMA PINE AND POPPA PINE:

We did!

LOGGER:

Trees don't talk.

POPPA PINE:

Not unless we've got something to say.

怎么回事？是谁在说话？

旁白：

树爸爸和树妈妈将它们的树枝叠在一起，形成一道密不透风的屏障，将树宝宝保护起来。

松树爸爸和松树妈妈异口同声地回答：

是我们在说话。

伐木工人：

树是不会讲话的呀。

松树爸爸：

---

adult *adj.* 成熟的
shield *v.* 保护；庇护

impenetrable *adj.* 不可进入的；穿不过的

MOMMA PINE:

And now we've got something to say.

Leave Baby Pine alone!

LOGGER:

I'm sorry. I didn't think. I just needed some room.

MOMMA PINE:

Isn't that always the *case*? Loggers always need a little room, so they chop down tiny, *defenseless* trees.

我们有话要说的时候就会讲话。

松树妈妈：

我们现在就有话要说。不要伤害我们的孩子！

伐木工人：

对不起，我并没有想要伤害你们的孩子，我只是需要些空间开始我的工作。

松树妈妈：

你们总是这样，不是吗？总是需要空间，就把一棵棵小树砍倒，小树又不能反抗。

---

case *n.* 具体情况；实情；事实　　defenseless *adj.* 不能自卫的；无防御的

LOGGER:

That's not true!

MOMMA PINE:

I am so angry I could just *smack* you.

POPPA PINE:

Look, we know why you're here, you, you. . . presto logger!

LOGGER:

I am not a presto logger. Where did you get that idea?

伐木工人：

不是这样的！

松树妈妈：

我实在太气愤了，真想给你一个耳光。

松树爸爸：

听着，我们知道你为什么来这儿，你，你……你不就是想把我们加工成燃料吗？

伐木工人：

不是的，你们怎么会这么想呢？

---

smack *v.* 用巴掌打；掴

MOMMA PINE:

Well, uh, we thought because all the trees . . .

POPPA PINE:

You know, the forest is gone almost *overnight*, and we just thought

that, you know, uh, just like that, presto! Presto log. We don't want

to be ground up into presto logs. We won't go!

LOGGER:

Well, I'm not going to take you if you don't want to go. But I

松树妈妈:

嗯，这个，我们会这么想是因为所有的树都……

松树爸爸:

你也看到了，整个森林一夜之间变得荒芜，所以我们认为……我们认为你们会把我们也砍掉，然后变成燃料。

我们不想变成木屑，我们不会离开这里的！

伐木工人:

好吧，如果你们不想离开这里，那就算了吧。但是我本以为你们是愿意成为圣诞树的，看来我错了。

---

overnight *adv.* 突然；一夜之间

always thought that you guys wanted to be Christmas trees. I guess I was wrong.

POPPA PINE:

Hey, hey, no rush here. I mean heh, heh! Christmas trees, you say?

NARRATOR:

Momma Pine *primps* her upper branches with her boughs.

MOMMA PINE:

You mean Christmas trees, as in lights and *tinsel* and *garland*?

松树爸爸：

喂，喂，别急着走啊，呵呵，你刚才说什么？成为圣诞树？

旁白：

松树妈妈开始用树干精心地打扮起上方的枝叶。

松树妈妈：

你是说我们会成为圣诞树吗？就是有彩灯、亮片，还有花环装饰的圣诞树？

伐木工人：

---

primp *v.* 打扮；修饰
garland *n.* 花环；花冠

tinsel *n.* (尤指圣诞节时装饰用的)光片

LOGGER:

Yeah. But if you guys don't want to go, I'll just be on my way.

MOMMA PINE:

No! No! Of course we're . . . we're *flattered* and all. This is the biggest of big for a tree. But what about Baby? We can't leave Baby.

LOGGER:

Look, I'm sorry about that. I wasn't thinking. The little Pine will be cared for and fed and watered. We'll let it sleep through the winter. Come spring, I'll be with it most every day. Baby's pine cones will grow an *entire* new forest full of castaway pines around here. And I

是啊，但是如果你们不想离开，我看我还是走吧。

松树妈妈：

不，不，我们当然想离开……这是我们的荣幸，是我们莫大的荣幸。但是我们的孩子怎么办？我们不能离开它啊。

伐木工人：

哦，这个很抱歉，之前我没考虑到这一点。放心吧，我们会细心呵护它的，让它在这个冬天里睡个好觉，春天到来时，我会每天陪伴着它。到那时，留在这的这些小松树就将长成一片茂密的森林。而且我保证，几年

---

flattered *adj.* 深感荣幸的   entire *adj.* 全部的；整个的

promise you, a few years from now, Baby will be a Christmas tree, too.

BABY PINE:

Hey, what's going on?

NARRATOR:

In *response*, the two older pines lock branches and begin to sing "Oh, Christmas Tree."

LOGGER:

May you all find the best in this, the season of snow. Happy holidays.

后，你们的宝宝也会成为圣诞树的。

松树宝宝：

喂，你们在说什么呢？

旁白：

树爸爸和树妈妈手牵手，开始唱起歌来："噢，圣诞树。"

伐木工人：

愿你们尽情享受这个飘雪的季节，圣诞快乐！

---

response n. (口头或书面的)回答；答复